WORDS THAT
HEAL TODAY

Books by Ernest Holmes

CREATIVE MIND

CREATIVE MIND AND SUCCESS

THE SCIENCE OF MIND

QUESTIONS AND ANSWERS (WITH ALBERTA SMITH)

NEW THOUGHT TERMS AND THEIR MEANINGS

MIND REMAKES YOUR WORLD (EDITED)

THIS THING CALLED LIFE

THIS THING CALLED YOU

Words
That Heal
Today

ERNEST HOLMES

DODD, MEAD & COMPANY
New York

Fifteenth Printing

Contents

WORDS THAT
HEAL TODAY

CHAPTER I

The Voice of God to Humanity

—————⁓—————

. . . and Jesus said, "Ask and ye shall receive."

IT WAS this tremendous claim on God that amazed both his friends and his enemies. He performed miracles as though they were the most ordinary experiences in human life. He made demands on an invisible Power that no other man before had dared to make, and this Power honored his demand.

This master mind was either the great exception or the great example. The claim he made on the universe was either made by one whom God had peculiarly endowed with spiritual power, or it is a claim that anyone can make with complete assurance, provided he first complies with the conditions laid down by the greatest spiritual genius of the ages.

We cannot compare the philosophy of Jesus with others. We cannot say he was this or that or something else. We can only say: here was a man who

3

found himself inseparable from God, eternal with God, forever in God. Conscious of his divinity, yet humble as he contemplated the infinite life around him, he spoke from the height of spiritual perception, proclaiming the deathless reality of the personal life, the continuity of the individual soul, the unity of the universal Spirit.

We find in him a heart of kindness, a mind of comprehension, an intellect of sincerity, a feeling of compassion. He was a lover of humanity. He knew it in its wisdom and folly, in its righteousness and mistakes. He had the spiritual vision to know that when God has made the pile complete everything that does not belong to the kingdom of good will be purged from it. He knew that the divine spark in all men must, somewhere, sometime, be fanned into a celestial blaze. He knew that good must eventually overcome evil, that the Kingdom of Heaven, which is at the center of our being, will become established at its circumference.

Jesus made heaven and earth meet. Sublime in his own spiritual completeness he had risen in joy, in calm serenity, to a lofty height whose vastness included all. It was his use of spiritual power his contemporaries could not understand. They thought of God as separate from man. They had not conceived of man in God and God in man. They had intellectually accepted a unity which was no unity at all but a duality in that it excluded themselves.

Jesus paid little attention to the political and economic conditions of his time. He was non-resistant toward them. He established the Kingdom of God within himself. But while he said, "My kingdom is not of this world," he also lived in conformity with the world of his time.

He did not condemn the religions of others because they were different from his. When his disciples asked him to rebuke those who were casting out devils without using his name, he answered, "He that is not against us, is for us." He measured sincerity against insincerity, letting sincerity be the victor. He did not exalt himself as a leader but said, ". . . everyone that exalteth himself shall be abased; and he that humbleth himself shall be exalted."

One thing is certain, we cannot find the key to this man's character by going to the ordinary locksmith. He had a pattern different from others. He viewed the universe as a spiritual system—not by and by, but here and now. He saw it, felt it, knew it, understood and experienced it.

Jesus believed in a spiritual truth which gives power over evil. He affirmed that God's Kingdom is here and now. His thoughts were so simple that we can easily overlook their profoundness. He was no splitter of words or phrases.

He spent no time in abstractions or what we are fondly likely to think of as "deep" and profound philosophies. We may study the teachings of other philosophers, whether ancient, medieval or modern, and we shall find that many of their phrases are meaningless, not so much spiritual perceptions as intellectual gymnastics. How refreshing to read the simple thoughts of one who had a direct perception of the spiritual universe here and now! In the words of Jesus are contained the depth and meaning of the many systems which are so difficult to follow.

Seeking a true interpretation of the teaching of the Master we should forget our dogmas and many of our personal opinions, and start with the simple proposition that Jesus knew what he was talking about. If we do this, we shall arrive at conclusions so stupendous that they shatter the imagination. We shall arrive at a concept of the Divine Presence so satisfying that it will become to us as the pearl of great price for which we would gladly exchange all we have that we may possess it. We shall arrive at such a magnificent concept of a universe of law and order that we shall know our faith and trust are placed in an immutability. And we shall have a feeling of personal relationship to this universe, a divine companionship with God. We shall come to know that all have one Father in heaven to which each may come in his own individual way and from which each may draw inspiration for his personal life.

Jesus gave us a simple and direct approach to God,

a method of prayer, which, if used intelligently and sincerely by a majority of the human race, could bring peace on earth and good will among men. Every man's life revolves around an inward searching of his mind for that which he senses by intuition. Could we surrender the intellect to this intuition, the results would be miraculous.

The Man of Wisdom tells us how to do this both simply and directly. It is in the simplicity of faith, through an inward awareness, that we approach the great Giver of life. He said when we pray we should enter our closet, close the door and pray to the Father who sees in secret. He did not tell us to do this as an escape or as a psychological release from tension. He said that when we talk with the Father in secret, the Father who sees in secret will reward us openly.

It is not because of many words that God hears, but because of much meaning. God knows what we have need of. A spiritual pattern of our being already exists in the Divine Mind. As we turn to this inward perfection, opening our consciousness to its influx, it responds by flowing through and manifesting itself in us. Its response is not only a response of love, it is equally the reaction of an immutable law of cause and effect. In simple trust, by direct faith and through complete acceptance, we should expect the Spirit to answer our prayers and reward us openly.

The Great Teacher tells us that when we forgive

we shall be forgiven; when we refuse to forgive we shall not be forgiven. We wish to feel that God loves us and forgives our mistakes. But if we block our own forgiveness by refusing to forgive others, how can we hope to be forgiven?

This may seem a strange teaching, and yet, measuring it from the standpoint of justice and of cause and effect, it is simplicity itself. If we are filled with hatred toward others how can love flood our being with its light? We have set up a barrier. Necessity demands that we forgive if we would be forgiven. When we forgive, holding no condemnation, judging no one, then our consciousness becomes a mirror reflecting that greater Consciousness which is the Mind of God and the Will of Love.

Jesus tells us that the real treasures of life are eternal. They belong to the Kingdom of God within us. These treasures cannot be corrupted, they do not corrode, thieves cannot break through nor steal them. It is in this sense that no one gives to us but ourselves and no one takes from us but ourselves.

No one could ask for a higher justice or a greater mercy. If we can believe in an inner integrity, an inward security of which no man can rob us, then instead of putting on sackcloth and ashes and spending our time lamenting, we shall anoint our heads with the oil of peace, don the robe of confidence, and wear the shoes of gladness.

Jesus, who knew all things, said that when we keep the eye single the whole body will be filled with light. Turning to the light we receive that light. But turning only to darkness even such light as we have will become dimmed. We cannot serve two masters. If we believe that evil is equal to good, or that wrong is equal to right, the mind becomes a house divided. We shall have to desert the one to serve the other. The mind cannot travel in opposite directions without disintegration.

It is difficult to think peace in the midst of pain, to rise to a consciousness of joy in the midst of grief, or to believe in good when evil seems the more apparent. Yet the one who knew declared that we cannot serve two masters. He was right. He did not say it is easy to serve but one master. We all know how difficult it is to turn from doubt to faith, yet this is what he tells us to do.

Being a lover of nature, he compared our lives to the lilies of the field and the fowls of the air. The fowls of the air neither sow nor reap, nor do they gather into barns, yet the eternal bounty feeds them. The lilies of the field neither toil nor spin, yet they are clothed in beauty. If God does this for birds and flowers, will He not do as much for us?

Have we really believed in the Father Jesus was talking about? If we have not, have we any justification for denying what might happen should we really believe in what the Great Wayshower taught? Here is the challenge he sets before us: do we really believe? Theoretically, we do. Practically, we do not. Such belief as we have is mixed with confusion, uncertainty and doubt. We pollute the stream of faith with our unbelief.

But there is an apparent paradox in the teaching of Jesus. After telling us to believe, to have faith, he states that we cannot add one cubit to our stature by taking thought. This appears to be a contradiction until we measure the subtlety of its meaning. Let us take an example from nature, as the Great Teacher so often did. There is a law of gravitation which holds all physical objects in place. Our thought does not change this law or our stature in it, but we can shift our position in this law. We have personal freedom within it, but the law is not changed by the use we make of it.

We may throw ourselves with complete reliance upon the laws of nature and they will respond if we use them correctly. Our belief neither created nor can it change natural laws. It merely changes our attitude toward them and therefore changes their reaction to us.

The Master told us to seek the Kingdom first, that everything else is added. He said that our thoughts and motivations should be attuned to the Spirit. We should practice the Presence of God.

This would be seeking the Kingdom; this would be finding the Truth; this would be uniting with God. Jesus, the great and divine artist, might have been talking to other artists, saying, "If you would create the beautiful, seek first the essence of beauty. It is from this essence that the beautiful flows."

Glorious is the idea of trust the Enlightened One lays before us. Take no thought for the morrow for each day is sufficient unto itself. In this passage the thoughtful will find a subtle depth of meaning, an allusion to that time which knows but one eternal day. Thinking of tomorrow is thinking of that which is not yet and which never can become. It is impossible to live in tomorrow. When tomorrow comes it will be today. In taking thought for today, tomorrow will take thought for itself. Today's actions produce tomorrow's results. If today's actions are noble, tomorrow's reactions also will be noble.

Much that Jesus said appears to lack sympathy until we realize that he was not only revealing a God of love but with equal clarity announcing a universal law. "Judge not that ye be not judged, for with what judgment ye judge ye shall be judged" means justice without judgment. There is no final *judge* in the universe. There is a final *justice*.

Justice is balance, equilibrium, compensation or retribution according to the use we have made of the law of cause and effect.

Jesus places the final judgment of the act in the act itself. This is complete impartiality, the highest degree of justice, a perfect balance. We are individuals. In the law of life nothing condemns us but ourselves, nothing saves us but ourselves. We are given this freedom. What goes from us can again return—not only can, it must.

This is difficult to accept because we like to project the blame for our own misdeeds into others, into society or destiny. We read the stars to see what fate holds in store. We like to feel that our destiny is outside ourselves. Jesus, the greatest of the great, cuts a swath through superstition and ignorance and draws a straight line between cause and effect, placing our inward thoughts at one end of this line and their external results at the other.

Our judgment of others becomes a judgment of ourselves. We must be judged by the very judgment with which we judge. This is hard to accept. Yet, common sense tells us it is an announcement of the integrity of a universe which no one can violate. If we think this through carefully the realization of its meaning will produce a healing, for we shall have discovered causation at the only point of contact with us where we could have any authority over it. Unless we are the arbiters of our own fate and the creators of our own destiny we could not be free. We should be automatons.

If life is "measure for measure," how careful we should be in our measuring. If we wish goodness to be measured back to us, we must measure it out. But we should not feel that we are bartering with the Almighty. There are no cosmic bargain counters. God's Kingdom has no favorites. It is a balance of love and law, of the personal and the impersonal. We are the personal, the Law of life is impersonal.

Jesus tells us to become as little children; that we should actually believe in God and live by faith and inspiration. It is this simplicity which eludes us. It is so direct, so spontaneous that we are likely to think of it only as a thing of faith and beauty—which it most certainly is—and to overlook its spiritual meaning.

Who would know God must be as God, for He who inhabits eternity also finds a dwelling place in His own creation. Standing before the altar of faith in the temple of life, one learns that he is an integral part of the universe and that it would be incomplete without him.

There is a Presence pervading all, an Intelligence running through all. There is a Power sustaining all, binding all into one perfect whole. The realization of this Presence, Intelligence, Power and Unity constitutes the nature of the mystic Christ, the indwelling Spirit, the Sonship of the Father. This is what Jesus knew. This is why he reveals Christ to us.

Jesus plunged beneath the material surface of things and found their spiritual cause. This cause he called God, or the Father. To this indwelling God he constantly turned for help, guidance and counsel. To him, God was an indwelling Reality, the Infinite Person in every personality. It was by the power of this Spirit that he lived. As Jesus, the man, gave way to the Divine Ideal, the human took on the Christ and became the voice of God to humanity.

It is written that Jesus was led of the Spirit into the wilderness, to be tempted of the devil. What does it mean to be led of the Spirit other than to follow our inner intuition? The Spirit is everywhere present, therefore, It must be at the center of our being as well as around us. The Spirit does not lead us as one man leads another, but through an inner urging of the soul. Jesus had fasted for forty days, found solace and comfort in conscious communion with the Spirit which was within him. Realizing that physical substance is but a symbol of the divine bread of life, he called this bread "the word that proceedeth out of the mouth of God."

One ancient commentator says that "devil" is a symbol of the illusory principle of evil, that which seems opposed to good, the not-self which is opposed to the true self. "Devil" stands for the negative rather than the positive viewpoint of life, and according to one of the greatest of the Christian theologians, denotes the absence rather than the presence of something. It was in this wilderness of thought that the intellect of Jesus, representing the human mind, conversed with the incarnation of Christ, God within him.

Again the devil took him up into the holy city and set him upon the pinnacle of the temple, representing spiritual power and a consciousness that through using this power he could perform such wonderful feats that the multitude would stand in awe before him, would look upon him as God.

This is the struggle that goes on between our inward consciousness of what is right and a personal desire for power. It was the decision of Jesus to use his spiritual power for the benefit of the world and not for personal gratification. As he did throughout his entire life, he was putting first things first, knowing that everything else is included within the Divine Kingdom.

He deliberately refused the kingdoms of this world because he had caught the vision of a heavenly kingdom. The lesser vision gave way to the greater. Often our more personal good must be surrendered to a larger good, to a more inclusive consciousness of life. If we are caught in the lesser, how can the greater come? Jesus could not have accepted the smaller vision. He had outgrown it. He threw it aside as unworthy his higher vision. He was able to say that God only should be served, God only should be worshipped.

At this moment of supreme renunciation it is written that angels ministered unto him. Whether we choose to accept this symbolically or literally is of no consequence, for it is its meaning we should search out. Every man is accompanied through life by a Divine Presence which is both universal and individual—universal in that It is an overshadowing Presence, individual in that It is an indwelling Spirit. Jesus penetrated the veil which is so thin between the seen and the unseen and opened his consciousness to an influx of spiritual strength.

This inward consciousness reflected itself in his physical being so that the hunger and thirst of the flesh were gratified by the bread and water of Spirit. Physical strength was restored and he descended from the mountain top of realization to minister to those who were without hope.

Vast multitudes followed him as they always follow those who give them back to themselves. Great spiritual teachers are those whose intellect and feeling have climbed the ladder of an inner awareness which all have but which few use. Because the same spiritual altitudes are within everyone, even though unscaled, all are able in some degree to understand

Jesus. It is in this sense that he reveals us to ourselves.

There is something contagious about spiritual insight. It envelops those who have it with an atmosphere of light, a consciousness of good, a feeling of security and peace. We should spend much time on the mountain top of spiritual vision if we would find the treasure of the Spirit. Descending from this spiritual altitude, we carry back with us, into the market place and the highways and byways of human endeavor, some echo of the beauty of that celestial palace which we have entered and where we have known that we were the guests of God. Did not the Master say, "In my Father's house are many mansions"?

CHAPTER II

Master of Men

AND Jesus went up into a mountain to commune with the Spirit, and when he descended he brought such a vision of God with him that the multitudes gladly followed. Looking up from their great need they saw one whose countenance shone, whose whole physical being radiated spiritual light and power. Out of his love and compassion he taught them, saying:

"Blessed are the poor in spirit: for theirs is the kingdom of heaven." Since there can be no poverty of the Divine, he must have been referring to an impoverishment of the human, which, having exhausted its small personal resources, finds itself cut off from the perennial source of all being. Jesus was the great awakener. Being conscious of the Divine Presence in all things, he was able to strike a corresponding awareness in others, to light the wick of their candles, which he knew ran deep into the oil of Spirit, from his own inward flame.

"Blessed are they that mourn: for they shall be comforted." Who has not mourned? We all seek the comfort of assurance, the blessedness of peace, the security of certainty. That our mourning shall be turned into joy and our grief into gladness, is one of the quests of humanity. Perhaps Jesus chose this word picture to teach us that when we gain a consciousness of the Kingdom of God our tears will be dried by gladness; that joy and happiness come to those who hunger and thirst after righteousness.

"Blessed are the meek: for they shall inherit the earth." This is difficult to understand. Yet, if we view life from the long run we find that the meek alone do really inherit the earth. Let us take the life of Jesus as the outstanding example of this. We so often think of him only as downtrodden, persecuted, despised and finally crucified. We think of him as one whose meekness was a plaything of the arrogant, scorned by the intellectual, cast out by those in power, persecuted and crucified by those whose love and adoration he should have received. Yet, of all men in history, Jesus has received more devotion, more adoration, more love and more gratitude than any hundred other persons who ever lived.

We read of the empire builders of the world, of the arrogant and scornful, but we do not think of them with love or admiration. They are not the ones we follow. We do not search out their thoughts, dwelling on every word they spoke. They are cast aside, lost in the backwash of human evolution. Those whom we love are the simple souls, the great prophets, those who loved humanity. Truly, the meek alone do inherit the earth.

But there was no false meekness about the teaching of this great man. He always spoke with authority. There was no quivering of the tongue, no hesitation in the thought, no stuttering of his words. There was no false humility in Jesus. Boldly but meekly he proclaimed the Kingdom. Awed before the grandeur of his sublime realization, he submerged all that was little into an all-inclusive concept of the Kingdom of God. More than all others Jesus does inherit the earth through the lives of countless millions.

"Blessed are they which do hunger and thirst after righteousness: for they shall be filled." Jesus taught a law of parallels. The spiritual universe was real to him, something to be immediately perceived and experienced. He often referred to the laws of nature and the heavenly kingdom as though everything we see is but an outpicturing of an invisible cause. As we hunger and thirst physically, so we hunger and thirst after righteousness, after a right relationship to that which the intuition feels and the intellect needs.

There are many forms of starvation, of which physical hunger is but the most external. We all have an emotional hunger for love, an intellectual yearning for knowledge, a spiritual craving for wholeness. Jesus, more than all others, knew that just as people hunger for bread and meat, for wine and water, so there is an equal hunger for the bread of life and the water of Spirit. It is only when this yearning is deep enough that the consciousness turns within and receives, simply and directly, this bread of life and fulfills the desire of the soul to return to its source, to find itself whole in God.

One of the principal teachings of Jesus was that just as our physical hunger can be appeased, so our spiritual appetite can be gratified. We need not wait. To the one who saw the whole, waiting was futile. The Kingdom is always at hand. It is present with us, it is within and around us. Waiting but delays the day of fulfillment.

It is one thing to affirm that the Kingdom shall come. It is quite another thing to affirm that the Kingdom already is here. Thus we find that the philosophy of Jesus was not a denial of the physical world. It was, rather, a denial that the physical is separated from the spiritual. The two are one. This was a new concept, as little appreciated then as now. To the spiritual vision of this emancipated soul everything in the physical world has a corresponding reality in Spirit, present here and now, waiting to be perceived.

"Blessed are the merciful: for they shall obtain mercy." Jesus taught a definite law of cause and effect, that action and reaction are equal, that finally the universe responds to us by corresponding with our mental attitudes toward it. We cannot hope to judge the possibility of life by single or even multiple experiences. If life is to have meaning we must view it from the standpoint of continuity. We can find no intelligent interpretation of life if we believe it begins with birth and ends with death, as though it were a strange interlude starting in nothing, moving to nowhere; as though oblivion itself had cast a shadow of illusion across its own nothingness, so soon to fall back into the void from which, through some mishap, it had come.

It is only when we view life from the standpoint of an expanding soul, destined forever to exist somewhere, that we can make either sense or sanity out of human experience. If we view life from the standpoint that each is an evolving soul, destined to live forever somewhere, we shall see that in the long run life must return to us that which we reflect into it. In the long run only the merciful can obtain mercy. Hate will beget hate and love will give birth to that which is lovely. Joy will find joy and peace join with peace.

There is an inward compensation to the soul even in temporary affairs. There is always an answering of the Spirit in the terms of our approach to It. This law of cause and effect obtains here, now, and through all eternity. Since we are eternal beings, we may as well start here and now. If we believe that ultimately we must reap *as* we have sown, then we can also believe that we shall reap *what* we have sown. We should be certain that we are sowing the seeds of love, of mercy and of peace.

We may not catch the full significance of this in a day, a year or perhaps in a lifetime, but unless we doubt the justice of the universe in which we live we may be certain that finally the fruit of action must return to us. If our thoughts and deeds have gone out to bless, they will bring back joy and comfort. If they have gone out to hurt, they will return with hurt until the time of redemption of our mistakes, until we turn from the false to the true, from fear to faith, from hate to love.

"Blessed are the pure in heart: for they shall see God." "Heart" stands for the innermost sanctuary of our being, the Temple of God within us. Therefore it is written that "as a man thinketh in his heart, so is he;" "God is enthroned in the heart;" "The issues of life flow forth from the heart," etc. If God is in everything, or manifest through everything, then God is in and through us. It is only as our hearts, our inward thoughts, are pure, unadulterated and simple, that we can perceive the same purity, the same perfection, in that which appears to be external to our consciousness.

The Spirit is not only pure *in* heart, It is the purity *of* heart. It is the purity which exists at the center of things. Nothing has ever happened to this purity. Its apparent obscurity is caused by the confusion of our own thought. This is where the healing must take place. This calls for painstaking self-training, bringing discord and ugliness under the control of the harmonizing Spirit.

The pure in heart see God, but this divine vision is *only* to the pure in heart. This suggests a process of purification, a purgatorial cleansing of consciousness through the alchemy of Spirit. It suggests the necessity of careful and prayerful thought control. We must take time to practice the Divine Presence, to purify our consciousness through the purging of everything that denies the fundamental peace and harmony.

All personal egotism and bigotry must be discarded. We must come to realize that it is ourselves we see reflected in others. A fundamental unity ties us together with inseparable bonds. It is impossible to be isolated. In union alone can we find peace, can we see perfection or maintain that purity of consciousness to which Jesus referred when he said that the pure in heart shall see God.

When we become pure in heart we become perfect in spiritual vision. It is then that the intellect falls back to the original purity of the Divine Pattern. When we find this pattern in ourselves we shall see it in others. We reach God in others by reaching out from God within the self. Always the God in others will respond to the God in us, but never beyond the level of our inward spiritual awareness. As this level rises higher and higher in our consciousness and conduct we find the same level in others. Deep must call unto deep and deep respond to deep. The pure alone can behold the pure. The pure in heart alone can see God.

"Blessed are the peacemakers: for they shall be called the children of God." God is peace. We enter this peace in such degree as we withdraw from confusion. But not to ourselves alone does this peace belong. The peace of God is universal, all-inclusive, all-embracing. This does not mean that everything should be reduced to sameness. Unity does not mean uniformity. Life has set the stamp of individuality upon everything, from a blade of grass to a person. There is unity at the center, variety at the surface. These variations are separate and distinct without being separated or isolated. Variety feeds on the unity in which it is rooted and expands through a consciousness of being one with the whole.

The simplicity and directness of the teaching of Jesus assailed the doctrines and dogmas of his day, as it does of ours. It contradicted the assumption of special authority delivered to a few and demanded that we find God at the center of everything. In a day when the priests had proclaimed themselves the sole keepers of the law, the only guide to eternal life, it remained for an unknown teacher to proclaim that every man is an inlet and may become an outlet to the Divine Nature. It was a spiritual and not an ecclesiastical authority which the Great Teacher was talking about. It was an inward awareness he pointed to, the immediate perception of one's union with God, a union which includes all people and all things.

It was this simple and direct approach to the Spirit that confounded those caught in form and ritual, in dogma and bigotry. Jesus tells us that heaven is within, that when we separate ourselves from confusion, doubt and fear, we shall find this heaven. It was an immediate awareness of the Spirit that he preached. This was startling to those who had deferred the day of at-one-ment to some mythical or mystical future. To Jesus the Kingdom of Heaven was eternally at hand. The reward of every right and true act already exists in the Kingdom of Good.

In the exalted concept of the Illumined One no weary journeyings of the soul were necessary to gain the heavenly Kingdom, no pain other than that produced through ignorance, no series of repeated incarnations dragging themselves out through endless eons of monotonous drabness. Jesus said: Open the door of your mind and the heavenly light will enter. Open it today! You could have opened it yesterday. You may defer the divine event until tomorrow. Some day, somewhere, you will open the door and the floodlights of eternal life will flow through you.

The Master's idea of the spiritual included the physical. The spiritual ought by every right to dominate the physical, to control it, to use it as a plaything of the soul. Even the immutable law of cause and effect was to Jesus as a plaything. He saw that new series of events could be introduced and old ones changed as a higher consciousness is brought to bear on them. Great is the reward in heaven, great is the activity of heaven upon earth, when our consciousness turns to the Divine Harmony, imbibes Its spirit and permits Its life to flow through us in thought and act.

To many of the ancients salt was a symbol of truth and wisdom. It was their custom to say, "Let your speech be savored with salt." When Jesus said, "Ye are the salt of the earth," he was referring to the consciousness of those to whom he had given spiritual instruction. As salt preserves, so their consciousness could preserve the world if the world would permit it. It could bring wisdom to the world.

But if their salt should lose its savor, then it would be of no value. Unless our spiritual powers are used they will avail us nothing. Nature always seems to say: "Use or lose; create or die"—not an eternal death, of course, but death to present realization. But when salt does not lose its savor, when wisdom speaks through knowledge, then it becomes a light unto the world.

Light is used as a symbol of truth. "And God said, Let there be light, and there was light" because God is light. This light, which proceeds from the Spirit, annihilating darkness, has been referred to as the Father of Lights. Jesus said that we are not cut off from the light in reality; that even in our ignorance the light still shines, whether or not we comprehend it; that at any moment our wicks may be relighted from the celestial flame itself. He told us that we should not put our light under a bushel; we should not cover or hide it. We should put it in a candle stick that it may give forth light to others.

"Candle stick" was a symbol of wisdom and love, bearing the light of truth. Thus we have a candle before the altar. The three-branch candle stick representing the trinity and the seven-branch signifying completion—the seven days of the week and the seventh year in which all debts were forgiven. Therefore, our candle is not to be covered but set in a candle stick that it may give light to all that are in the house.

"House" has two meanings, one individual, the

other universal. The Great House and the Small House. "But Christ as a son over his (God's) house, whose house we are if we hold fast our boldness and the glorying of our hope." The scripture has many references to the House of God and the house of man, to the individual and the Universal. It always means the Father and the son. The individual house must be lighted with the universal or eternal light.

Jesus tells us to let our light so shine that we may glorify our Father which is in heaven. The son must glorify the Father in order that the Father may further glorify the son. The law of action and reaction will be equal. It is only as we accept the gift of life that it can be received. The gift itself is made from the foundations of the universe. God's nature has never changed. It ever presses against us but we must accept it. Accepting it, following its light and living in its glow, we glorify the indwelling Spirit which is God in us, the Universal operating on the plane of the individual. The two are one. This one is God.

We are not to suppose that the influx of Divine Light extinguishes our individual lamps. It but accentuates their glow. There is nothing in the teaching of Jesus that calls for the annihilation of the individual stream of consciousness. He merely includes it in that greater consciousness which he

called the Kingdom of God. It was not his idea that
we be lost in Divinity, but that we be found in God.

There is a vast difference between these two
thoughts. One is annihilation, the other is inclusion.
One is absorption, the other is immersion. Jesus
taught inclusion and immersion, not annihilation or
absorption. He had reconciled unity with multi-
plicity, oneness with variation. He saw God in everything—the wind and the wave—Divine Intelligence
dominating nature; love flowing through all its
forms; beauty, harmony, law and order binding
everything together in one cohesive unity.

This concept is so tremendous that it staggers the
imagination. Yet we should not be lost in its mere
abstraction, but rather, realize that our individual
lives can be so joined with the Eternal Glory that
we think the thoughts of God after Him and do the
works of the Spirit through the power of some divine
grace which waits our acceptance.

Thus the Wayshower said that he did not come to
destroy the law or to deny the prophets. He came
not to destroy, but to fulfill. The prophets had proclaimed that someone would come who would speak
forth the Divine Nature in word and in deed. Jesus
was such an one. In him all prophecies were fulfilled,
not because he was different from others, but because
he was conscious of that Divine Nature which is in
all people.

He conformed to human customs and laws when they did not contradict principles. He knew that while we are in this world we must be a part of it and not apart from it. He carried his religion and spiritual perception into everyday living, making it a practical philosophy of life rather than a vague spiritual idealism. We would do well to follow his example and seek to connect life with living and spiritual power with human performance.

Jesus knew that the sick must be healed, the hungry fed, that taxes must be paid to support governments, that law and order must prevail. He was not one who took away, but one who added to. He was one who saw God in everything and believed that through faith in God we may joyously enter into the fullness of living.

The followers of the Master, being human and much like the rest of us, loved prestige and power, and so they asked him, "Who is the greatest in the kingdom of heaven?" No doubt they hoped he would answer, "I am the greatest and you, my disciples, are next." They must have been surprised at his answer, for he said that the greatest in the Kingdom is the one who accepts God in childlike faith, in simple and direct trust. The natural child has no sense of shame, no burden of guilt, no consciousness of rejection. The natural child loves everyone and expects everyone to love it, puts forth its hand in trust and enters into the zest of living with abandonment and joy.

Jesus loved children because he himself had gained this childlike trust in God. How often in our complexities we turn back in thought to the time of childhood when there were no burdens, no fears, no doubts, and long again to return to our lost paradise. But the Master tells us it is not necessary that we actually return to physical and mental childhood. What we should do, if we wish happiness, peace and a sense of security, is to turn in childlike faith and confidence to the heavenly Father who withholds no good from us. We may recapture the dream of youth if we follow the example of Jesus and realize that we belong to the universe and that it belongs to us. We are one with it.

Indeed, much of the purpose of modern applied psychology is to carry the adult back to the innocence of childhood and bring the spontaneous reactions of childhood into the adult experience. The success of this method rests entirely on whether or not this is done. It is a proposition so simple that most people fail to grasp its spiritual significance.

Jesus understood this perfectly. He knew that the average adult is filled with confusion, fear and doubt, with a sense of guilt and rejection, which come from a consciousness of not being wanted. He knew, better than the modern psychologist, how to restore this lost paradise. His method was so simple, so direct—just to become as a little child in our thinking about God; to accept life, to believe, to bring all our fear, uncertainty and weakness into the strength, the certainty and the assurance which alone come through communion with the Spirit.

Because our reactions to life are primarily mental he said that if our eye offend us we should pluck it out, or if our hand offend us we should cut it off. He said that our communication should be, "Yea, yea" and "Nay, nay."

Of course, we should not take this literally, as though in ordinary conversation all we should do would be to say, "Yes" and "No." But we can interpret it from the standpoint that we are either affirming life or denying it. We are either accepting it or rejecting it. We have faith or fear, hope or despair; we experience good or evil, love or hate; we live in heaven or in hell. In our conversation and thought we are either saying "Yes" or "No" to life.

It is from this viewpoint that these passages should be interpreted. Jesus is telling us to live, think and talk affirmatively. That which adulterates the truth, that which denies the truth, separates us from the good we would experience. This negation of good we call evil.

Moses taught the harsh doctrine of an eye for an eye and a tooth for a tooth. He presented a law of justice, a law of action and reaction. Jesus completes this teaching by saying that we should not resist evil, that we should love our enemies, bless them that curse us, do good to those who hate us, and pray for those who persecute us. He knew what modern psychology has disclosed, that the hate we bear others harms us the most; that only as we practice non-resistance to evil do we overcome it.

He does not imply that non-resistance means acquiescence, that it means we accept negative conditions or circumstances as being right. Non-resistance means non-combativeness. Instead of contending against evil we should think good; instead of fighting the devil we should worship God; instead of being overcome by grief we should enter the joy of living. Turning from lack, want and limitation, we should become conscious of divine abundance, the overflowing of the substance of Spirit into our personal experience.

The Great Revelator said that if we would be as the children of our Father which is in heaven we must realize that the eternal Giver is also the eternal Forgiver. This in no way makes evil equal to good. We enter into good as we forsake evil. When we are turned to the light, all shadows are cast backward, but when we turn from the light the shadows are in front of us.

On a certain occasion Jesus was accused of eat-

ing with publicans and sinners. He was called glut-
tonous and a wine bibber. Since he saw fit to answer
this accusation, it is well to consider the meaning of
his words: "But wisdom is justified of her children."
Life is not separated from living. Fellowship with
others is not separated from the Kingdom of Heaven.
The Kingdom of Heaven on earth is a community of
souls living together in a brotherhood of man, under
the Fatherhood of God.

Jesus was no recluse. One who could turn water
into wine and multiply loaves and fishes need not
sit around with a begging bowl. Neither did he
teach a stern severity in the mastery of the Spirit.
He taught that all things, rightly used, belong to
the kingdom. Jesus was not morbid. He was a
happy and triumphant soul, proclaiming that the
Kingdom of God is at hand. Mingling with the multitude, being one with them and entering into their
joy and sorrow, their laughter and dancing, their
prayer and song, he was able to bring to them the
true meaning of the sacrament of Spirit—the bread of
life and the wine of wisdom—the bread for substance,
the wine for joy.

In order to be righteous we sometimes believe we
must forsake all pleasure, living only in meditation
and prayer. But he who understood all things taught
a balanced life. He sang no hymn of hate to his enemies, nor did he tell his friends that they should for-

sake the joy of living. Rather, he said that we should live always as though the table of life were spread by a Divine Hand. The very hairs of our heads are numbered. God knows what we have need of day by day and is able and willing to supply these needs. He tells us to live a glad, spontaneous and joyful life, a life of trust and faith.

And he was right. How can we love God, whom we have not seen, unless we love our fellowman whom we have seen? How can we enter into a Kingdom which is not here? How can we commune with a God who refuses to answer today? How can we separate life from living? We should live as though our food were Divine Substance, as though the water we drink were the flow of Life from the perennial fountain of all being.

The Sadducees and Pharisees, the scribes and chief priests and the elders of the people played an important role in the drama of the life of Jesus. They were irritants, always confronting him with the question of by what authority did he speak or act. His response was so subtle that they could not follow it. They had no mental equivalent of the spiritual universe he was talking about. They had no concept of mental and spiritual laws, a knowledge of which was commonplace to this master mind. They had not tuned in to that Kingdom of Heaven whose atmosphere was natural to him. They lacked the deep feeling necessary to a penetration of the inner life. Their equivalents were objective rather than subjective. They were of the intellect, not of the spirit.

On one of the occasions when they were questioning Jesus he spoke to them in a parable, saying there was a certain man who had two sons. He asked one of them to work in the vineyard. This son refused, but afterward, relenting, he went forth to work. Asking the second son to go, his answer was, "I go, sir, and went not." Jesus asked them which of the sons was doing the will of his father. It is self-evident that the son, who, though he refused to go, actually went, was doing the will of the father rather than the one who said he would go but who remained in the house.

It is now known that when the intellect affirms what the imagination denies it will be the imagination that wins and not the intellect. This does not exclude the idea that the intellect can gradually remold our emotional responses to life and the Great Teacher was pointing out that it is the deep inward feeling and response to life that really counts. He was uncovering the well-springs of creative imagination that exist at the center of everyone's life. He knew, as all must learn, that there is a place deep in everyone's mind that acts as an inlet to the Divine Nature, just as the intellect can and should be a constructive outlet for those deep emotional yearnings that we all have.

Speaking to the misinformed intellect, Jesus said, "Verily I say unto you, that the publicans and the harlots go into the kingdom of God before you." He told them that "the kingdom of God shall be taken from you and given to a life bringing forth the fruits thereof." The fruits of the Kingdom belong to those who gather them. Beauty exists for the one who beholds it. The wine of life is made from the fruit of the vine rooted in the mother of all creation.

The Wise One likens the harlots, the publicans and sinners who repent to that feeling toward life, which, though often chaotic, is still deep and sincere. It was the great heart of Jesus that gave him this divine compassion, a tolerance even for our mistakes, a spirit of forgivingness which binds up our self-inflicted wounds with the balm of renewed hope and faith.

The Pharisees, being afraid of Jesus, took council among themselves, seeking to entangle him. And so they asked, "Is it lawful to give tribute unto Caesar? . . ." But Jesus perceived their wickedness, and said, "Why tempt me, ye hypocrites? Show me the tribute money." Taking a penny which they brought to him he asked, "Whose is this image and super-scription?" They answered, "It is Caesar's." And

Jesus replied by saying, "Render therefore unto Caesar the things which are Caesar's; and unto God the things that are God's." He knew there must be law and order in this world as well as in the next, that contracts must be made and kept, and that human relationships must be inviolate. We must render unto Caesar that which belongs to Caesar, but also unto God that which belongs to God.

So subtle was this answer that they went away confused but marvelling at his wisdom. On the same day they again came to him with their net of intellectual intrigue and asked him how it would be in heaven with a man who had had several wives in this world—who would be his wife in heaven? Disregarding their small and meaningless controversy, "Jesus answered and said unto them, Ye do err, not knowing the scriptures, nor the power of God. For in the resurrection they neither marry, nor are given in marriage, but are as the angels of God in heaven. But as touching the resurrection of the dead, have ye not read that which was spoken unto you by God, saying, I am the God of Abraham, and the God of Isaac and the God of Jacob? God is not the God of the dead, but of the living."

God is life. Life cannot produce death. Death is but the shifting of a scene, the moving from one place to another, an impatient gesture of the soul as it seeks freedom. He is not a God of the dead because He is life "and will not suffer His holy one to see corruption." There is life and nothing but life. "I have come that they might have life, and that they might have it more abundantly." Since God is Life He can neither conceive of nor will death. This idea does not exclude physical dying or physical disintegration. It is not this flesh or this blood that enters into the next plane of our evolution. It is the mind, the soul and the consciousness that are eternal, inviolate, indestructible.

As usual, they had no answer to such divine wisdom, but turning to another technique asked, "What is the greatest commandment in all the law and from all the prophets?" Jesus replied by saying that to love God with our whole hearts and minds and souls is the first great commandment, "and the second is like unto it; Thou shalt love thy neighbor as thyself. On these two commandments hang all the law and the prophets." To love God and to love our neighbor as ourselves means to see God in everything and to include everyone in one divine unity. On this admonition of the Master hangs the meaning of all divine law, all spiritual prophecy and all true revelation.

There is no merely individual good. Good is universal. There is no exclusive salvation. All the good there is belongs alike to each. When we try to use this good exclusively we find it temporarily withdrawn, as though by the very hand of God. But, including others, we find our own good multiplied.

So perfect and commanding was the answer of Jesus that "no man was able to answer him a word." Having summed up the whole meaning of life in his teaching of the unity of man with God and the unity of man with man, he added the necessity of love and faith, of fellowship with the human and with the Divine, of the binding of all creation back into one vast spiritual system. He had reached the apex of all possible intellectual and emotional conclusions. With decisive logic and a depth of feeling which penetrated the hidden meaning of things he had drawn a picture so complete that nothing could be taken away and nothing need be added.

On a certain sabbath Jesus was walking through a corn field and he ". . . began to pluck the ears of corn, and to eat." The Pharisees had a law which said that no one should pick corn on the sabbath day, therefore they chose this occasion to censure him. His reply was that the son of man is Lord even of the sabbath, and that David, when he was hungry, had entered the house of God and eaten the shew-bread. And now comes this simple statement: "But I say unto you, that in this place is one greater than the temple." This one who is greater than the temple and Lord even of the sabbath is the Spirit within, the Lord of life.

It would be well to look into what is meant by the temple. The first temple was a portable tent which the children of Israel used in their wanderings, setting it up as a place of worship wherever they were. The second temple was built of wood, the third of precious stones. The last temple was called "a temple not made with hands, eternal in the heavens." It was this temple to which Jesus referred—the temple of God, the secret place of the most High within us. It is here that we abide under the shadow of the Almighty. This temple is the inner sanctuary of our spiritual being, the Lord of life, Lord even of the sabbath day. It is that which is beyond form and ritual, that which is nothing less than the Spirit in us.

Jesus said that had the Pharisees realized the true meaning of this temple they would have had mercy rather than sacrifice. When we enter the true temple, abiding in its secret place, the necessity for external sacrifice ceases. For the external act is not necessary to our real being, even though it often is necessary to our becoming. The search after truth is not truth. When we find what we are searching for the search ends, for the search ends with the finding. The Pharisees should have known this. Had they known it they would have realized the true significance of sacrifice. Condemnation, judgment and unkindness would have gone. After groping through the darkness, when the light comes we should abide in that light in whose presence darkness has neither power nor reality.

They asked Jesus if it were lawful to heal on the sabbath. He answered by asking if they on the sabbath would rescue a sheep that had fallen into a pit; if it were not lawful to do good at any time. And then he demonstrated the truth of his words by healing a withered arm. The Great Teacher coupled spiritual awareness with a consciousness of spiritual power. He placed no limitation on the possibility of using this spiritual power. He never doubted its response and he used this power wherever there was a need.

On another occasion the Pharisees and Sadducees, hoping to catch Jesus in a trap which the subtlety of their minds had laid for him, asked that he show them a sign from heaven. Comprehending their thought, he said, "When it is evening ye say it will be fair weather, for the sky is red; and in the morning it will be foul weather today, for the sky is red and lowering." He was using an illustration from natural law to point to its equivalent in the realm of mind and spirit.

All laws of nature converge. There must always be a correspondence between the objective and the subjective, between the seen and the invisible. If the Pharisees and Sadducees had known what their own spiritual doctrines taught they would have been able to read the book of life in mountain and vale, in stone and running brook.

" . . . give alms of such things as ye have; and, behold, all things are clean unto you." This is a repetition of the story of the boy who brought a few loaves and a few fish that Divine Love might multiply his scant store through the pattern of faith which he presented to his lord and master. In other words, the Master is saying: Use the talent you possess today. You have some love, some kindness, some faith, some belief in God. Let this be the pattern today. Bring such talents as you have, use them, and they will be multiplied.

We all are waiting for something to happen that will free us from bondage and give us more life. We are waiting for some external event, the advent of some teacher who will show us the way, not realizing that he has already come, written his lines on the pages of history, and departed, leaving behind a code of spiritual ethics and a law of conduct, the following of which alone can free us from our self-created bondage.

What simplicity! And what kindness! The compassion of this great soul who knew our frailties, who understood our physical and mental diseases, and who out of his great heart of love said, in effect: "Take the pattern you already have. Use the best you know. Forget the rest and leave the answer to God. Let good multiply what you bring to it. Let the love you have for each other be compared to that greater love of God to all. Remove your weak and flickering candle from under the bushel of obscurity with which you have covered it. Let your light shine and you will soon find that it mingles with that heavenly light which lighteth every man's path to the Kingdom of Good." Jesus never left anyone in despair.

CHAPTER III

The Great Presence and the Great Law

WHEN Jesus said that we must agree with our adversary lest we be cast into prison, he was using a figure of speech in reference to our self-imposed limitations. Hate casts the one who indulges in it into a prison of his own making, just as fear casts one into the prison of doubt. We build the walls that enclose us. We lock the door, shutting ourselves from the light.

God has built no walls, locked no doors and cast none in prison. All prisons are self-created. And even in the cell of fear, on the cot of unbelief, in the dampness of morbidity and doubt, or the stale atmosphere of confusion, even here the divine light penetrates. At the top of our cell is a door which even we could not close. It is through this door that the Spirit enters.

Love is the great lodestone of life. If we have faith, confidence and love, we shall be led by a pathway the intellect does not know. We shall be led of the Spirit. Trusting and trying, suffering any temporary setback without losing vision, we shall make progress. Though our hands tremble and our feet falter, they shall be made strong. Though our vision fail, it shall be restored. Faith, half lost, will be regained through trust.

It will be easier to understand the teaching of Jesus if we come to see the two fundamental propositions of his philosophy. First, God is Spirit, Infinite Person, Universal Presence. This Divine Presence is the Parent Mind, present everywhere, just as life is everywhere present. Being present everywhere, life is present within us. There are no vacuums in the Divine Mind. The Divine Presence is warm, colorful and personal, immediately responding to us. To this we should add the other great concept of Jesus: the universe is also a government of law. If this were not so the universe would be a vast chaos, which is unthinkable.

Let us call these two great realities Divine Person and Divine Principle. In our concept of Divine Principle we should include all the laws of nature, not overlooking the fact that there are laws of mind also. Let us think of the Law of Mind in action as we think of other laws of nature, as something to be used by our thought and faith. This is why Jesus said, "What things soever you desire . . ." He was not mentioning big or little, hard or easy, long or short. He was making a blanket statement about the law of cause and effect.

He said that not one jot nor one tittle of this law can be destroyed. The universe is a universe of love, governed by laws of justice, of balance, of equilibrium. Whoever seeks to break these laws will suffer correspondingly. "He shall be called the least in the kingdom of heaven." But whoever follows the law shall be called the greatest. The universe is just, without judgment.

The Master was not particularly condemning anyone. He was merely announcing the greater good. He was trying to show that life is from within, out. While Moses said that we should not kill, Jesus proclaimed that we should not even think evil. He tells us that it is of little avail to lay a gift on the altar while we hold enmity toward others. First we must become reconciled with our brother. The gift must be from the heart and not from the intellect alone.

How often we wish to be loved without loving, to be forgiven without forgiving, to receive without giving! This is impossible. Jesus, more than a sentimentalist, saw the universe as love acting through law. He explained that every mistake must bring with it a just retribution and every right act an equal compensation. We cannot expect the universe to be divided against itself. It is always life-giving, always love-bearing, always fruitful of good. It is not a destroyer, but a builder.

"Ye cannot serve God and mammon." What did the Great Wayshower mean by this statement? He had already told his disciples that they must keep their eye single to the truth, that a house divided against itself cannot stand. Are we not trying to walk two ways at once? Do we not divide our attention between good and evil? Surely we try to serve both God and mammon. Jesus explained that the law of our being cannot be violated. "And it is easier for heaven and earth to pass than for one tittle of the law to fail."

Love wills life and life operates through law. The fundamental laws of our being are harmony, love and beauty. Whatever we do that contradicts these laws automatically draws a prison wall of limitation around us until the day of redemption through the reunion of our lives with the Spirit. Jesus said that our righteousness must exceed that of the scribes and Pharisees if we wish to enter into the Kingdom now. It is not merely an announcement of the law of life, but the doing of the will of love that brings us into the Kingdom of God. The announcement of the law of life is an act of the intellect. The doing of the will of love is a consecration of the soul.

It was the mission of Jesus to proclaim justice as well as wisdom, and law as well as love. The idea of justice is softened by the realization that because the law of life is just and cannot be broken, when we reverse our position in it, automatically we shall provide the channels for our freedom.

No sane person could ask for a fairer basis upon which to build. Nor could justice or common sense deny the necessity of suffering, through misdeed, until all wrong is swallowed up. Redemption comes from the turning of our whole being to that which alone can give life.

Paul, next to Jesus the greatest teacher of love and law, tells us that all things can be accomplished through the law of good if we have faith, hope and love. "Now the God of hope fill you with all joy and peace." Paul speaks of the God of hope, the God of patience and the God of consolation, and says that when we enter into unity with the Spirit we shall find that the God of peace will be with us. He holds up a dazzling vision, that through hope, expectation, faith and right action, through love for others and patience with ourselves, finally we shall unify with Christ.

Like the Master, Paul had found the way to peace of mind, which he said was a consciousness of unity through love. Like the Blessed One, Paul understood the frailties of the human mind and condemned no one because of them. He merely said: Try to do everything as though you were doing it unto God. In the long run you won't make many mistakes and the ones you have made will be wiped out. Jesus had referred to God as the Divine Giver and the Divine Forgiver. Paul referred to the heavenly Father as a God of consolation and compassion.

The conflict in our lives can be resolved only through a deep and abiding sense of security in the universe. This comes as we find our lives hid with Christ in God. Paul said that no matter what trials or tribulations, or how serious our errors, there is a light within which leads back to the central flame of our being, in whose light there can be no darkness.

He tells us not to grieve the Spirit, but, putting all bitterness away, walk in love, in peace and in happiness. He suggests that this is a process of awakening as though we were asleep to the deep realities of our being—a deep sleep from which we must be awakened as Jesus awoke Lazarus. When we awake, Paul says, we shall no longer walk "as fools but as wise," we shall "redeem the time and the days of evil," suggesting that negative sequences of cause and effect are redeemed when we awake to that fullness of time which is the eternal present of the Spirit.

It is impossible to read the thoughts of Jesus and Paul without realizing that their philosophy is based on the concept of the absolute supremacy of Spirit, here and now—a supremacy which can redeem our experiences in time and create new ones out of time. In this way time and experience are lifted up, are redeemed from the bondage of ignorance to the glorious freedom of Christ.

Neither Jesus nor Paul denied the reality of the world in which we live. What they affirmed was that this world is subject to its creator. That which creates can re-create. That which creates makes things out of itself by itself becoming what it makes. This creative agency which makes all things is absolute. There is nothing which it cannot do or undo. There is no circumstance which limits it. It has no otherness, no enemy and no law which can contend against it.

There may be many laws of limitation but *the* Law of God is limitless. We may have used the law of life to produce bondage, but since the law itself is freedom, when we subject our bondage to its freedom we are no longer bound. We have redeemed our time and brought it under subjection to that which is timeless. When we do this, that which is timeless creates for us a new sequence of time in which liberty appears instead of bondage. The whole process is reversed.

Moses and other prophets of old had hurled threats against the wrong-doer—a God of law sending thunderbolts or showering blessings. Jesus, who said that he came not to destroy but to fulfill, added to this concept of an overdwelling justice the thought of an indwelling Presence; the overdwelling and indwelling are one and identical—"The highest God and the innermost God is one God." This God is love as well as law.

Later, the Apostle Paul expressed the same thought in these words: "Though I speak with the tongues of men and of angels, and have not charity, I am become as sounding brass, or a tinkling cymbal." Unless there is love in the heart the tongue, howsoever eloquent, must have a metallic sound. It is when there is deep sincerity and an even deeper love that the intellect becomes the servant of the Spirit. Paul tells us that the gift of prophecy, the understanding of mysteries and the acquisition of all knowledge is as nothing compared to love. Even the faith that can move mountains, without love, is of no avail.

"And though I bestow all my goods to feed the poor, and though I give my body to be burned, and have not charity, it profiteth me nothing." It is when the self goes with the gift that it becomes an offering of love. The intellect and heart must go hand in hand. The altar of faith is profaned unless the gift laid on it is one of love. Nothing can profit us except it be of the nature of love. Though we burn the body or feed the poor or speak with angelic tongues, and have not love, there is no profit in any of it.

"Charity suffereth long, and is kind." Love never envies, does not vaunt itself, is not puffed up. It is this kind of love that is the fulfilling of the law of righteousness. Laws in themselves are but mechanical forces, and, being mechanical, can harm as well as aid. Should we bring every law in nature under subjection and learn to control all physical forces and use them without love, we should destroy ourselves. Love only is the fulfilling of the law, bringing its use to those high purposes that bind us back to the heart of the universe. Love waits for the fulfillment of the law. It is kind and does not envy. It seeks not its own and thinks no evil.

Love cannot seek its own as though it were separated from others. We are universal at the source and any act which tends to isolate us from our source tends to separate us from our Divine Nature. Because all are rooted in one life, any attempt to arrive at a good which is not shared is an attempt to isolate us from good itself. It is in this sense that love seeks not its own, is not puffed up, has no envy and knows no jealousy.

"And now abideth faith, hope, charity, these three; but the greatest of these is charity." Faith is good, hope is good, but love alone reveals the Divine. Following the guidance of Divine Love we finally come to know ourselves and each other as we already are known in the Spirit. Our intellect, emotion and will must become subject to love before they can follow the pathway of its light back to the central flame of the self-existent Cause.

Paul, like Jesus, expounding the two basic principles of reality—God as love, and the universe as law—said that the law "will render to every man according to his deeds" and "there is no respect of persons with God. For as many as have sinned without law shall also perish without law: and as many as have sinned in the law shall be judged by the law." This is a definite statement of the law of cause and effect working impersonally, both for those who believe in it and those who do not.

The law of life itself is a doer and not a knower. The Apostle shows that ignorance of the law excuses no one from its effect, while a knowledge of it leads to beneficial results. The operation of this law is at the center of our being, both as thought and as judgment. Paul mentions this when he says, "In the day when God shall judge the secrets of man. . . ."

Like Jesus, he warns that we be not hearers only but that we become doers of the law. "Thou therefore which teachest another, teachest thou not thyself." And he explains that when the righteous use the law unrighteously, they receive no beneficial results, but when the unrighteous use the law righteously, they will be benefited. "Therefore if the uncircumcised keep the righteousness of the law, shall not his uncircumcision be counted for circumcision?" He is not a true follower of Christ who acts outwardly for the sake of the act, but he is righteous whose "circumcision is that of the heart, in the spirit, and not in the letter." In this same sermon Paul said that God is a God of both Jew and Gentile, "seeing it is one God" which justifies all.

Paul had a complete acceptance of the law as an impersonal arbiter of fate. He said that our faith does not create the law, it uses it. "Do we then make void the law through faith? God forbid; yea, we establish the law." Faith does not create the law of righteousness, it establishes it in our experience. The collective faith of the human race cannot establish a false truth since there can be no such thing as a false truth. When everyone believed the world was flat it remained round. But one man who understood its roundness established this roundness in human experience.

The essence of Paul's teaching was a repetition of the thoughts of Jesus. He tells us that even love cannot excuse us from the effects of the wrong use of the laws of life. We are automatically punished until the law is used through love. It is then, and then only, that the just can hope to live by faith.

There is nothing fatalistic about this. Jesus plainly taught that we can break any chain of cause and effect our own misdeeds have created if we turn from these misdeeds. Therefore, the same law that closed our prison doors, reversed, can open them. Freedom and bondage are two ways of using one law. This is what Moses meant when he said, "Behold, I set before you a blessing and a curse; a blessing if ye obey the commandments, a curse if ye disobey the commandments."

Paul continues in this thought when he says, "For as many as are of the works of the law are under the curse . . . Christ hath redeemed us from the curse of the law" and "the just shall live by faith." Through turning in faith to good we pass out of the curse which the misuse of the law has laid upon us, into a new freedom which the law of itself was not able to give but which Christ in us, our true Sonship, reveals.

The Apostle explains that the law of itself, being merely a mechanical law of cause and effect, cannot bring salvation any more than the law of electricity could. Even the love of God cannot change the law of life. Divine Love and Infinite Wisdom could not create us as spontaneous individuals without letting us alone to discover ourselves. In the process of self-discovery we misuse the law of cause and effect. This is our sin or mistake. It is through these mistakes that we learn how to use the law of life rightly.

"Wherefore the law was our schoolmaster to bring us into Christ, that we might be justified by faith." This does not mean doing away with the law, for Paul asks, "Is the law then against us? God forbid." Law is necessary even to the harmony of heaven.

"But after that faith is come, we are no longer under a schoolmaster" for we are "the children of God by faith in Christ Jesus." As we come into conscious union with the Spirit and use the law of life in love and faith, the very law that once bound will free us.

Emancipation comes not by doing away with the law but by bringing it under subjection to the indwelling Christ. And because we are all children of God, sooner or later all will bring the law under subjection to Christ. "For as many of you as have been baptized into Christ have put on Christ." Putting on Christ means becoming actively and consciously aware of our Divine Sonship through love. And when this love has come, "there is neither Jew nor Greek, there is neither bond nor free, there is neither male nor female," but we are all "heirs according to the promise." This promise is not a material covenant that God has made with man but the inevitable covenant which life automatically makes with its creation.

It was the great mission of Jesus to tell us that we are in partnership with God. In this partnership there must be two signatures—God's, written in the invisible and spiritual laws of our being, and our own, written in our thoughts and acts. God has kept His contract with us. The Great Teacher tells us how to keep our contract with God. He tells us how it is to be fulfilled and what we may expect as a reward of right thought and act. He also tells us what to expect when we do not fulfill our contract.

This contract is between God and ourselves, between the Universal and the individual, between a heavenly Father and His earthly son. And the contract reads that the Party of the First Part, which is God, has agreed to give to the Party of the Second Part, which is man, eternal life, everlasting peace, blessedness, security, happiness and perfection, provided the Party of the Second Part fulfills his contract, which is to receive these divine gifts in the spirit in which they are made and through the law of their being, which is love.

God is life, God is love, God is wisdom, God is goodness. The divine necessity demands that we follow the nature of this life, love, wisdom and goodness, imbibe its spirit and pattern our lives after its perfection. Consequently, Jesus tells us that in fulfilling our part of the contract we must keep our light burning. We are not to put it under a bushel, but on a candle stick, keeping our eye single to this light that the whole body may be full of light.

Here again we find a veiled teaching, beautifully and kindly stated, but with a certain stern necessity attached to it. Jesus was more than a sentimentalist. Always we find a thread of law running through his teaching of love. The universe is a cosmos and not a chaos. There is no anarchy in the Spirit. Cause and effect govern everything.

Jesus uses the expression of keeping the eye full of light, comparing the eye to the mind. When our thinking responds to divine goodness, peace, joy and love, to givingness as well as to the idea of receiving, then the body will be filled with light. There will be calmness and peace at the center of our thought and in every direction we turn, upon whatever person or object our thought rests, blessing will follow. If our eye is divided between light and darkness, the result will be a mixture of good and evil.

Surely we should carefully study the instructions which the great Defense Attorney for the Kingdom of God has written for us. These instructions are so simple that we fail to grasp their profoundness and the subtlety of their meaning. Our lives have been built too much on the supposition that we are left alone to buffet our way through life, to beat down every opposition, to contend against every adversary. The conditions that have gathered around us have mounted to such gigantic proportions that the eye becomes filled with darkness. Yet, by some divine hope, some faith which we did not implant in ourselves, by some spiritual intuition we did not put there, we know there is a way, a truth and a life. And so we have never completely lost hope.

It was this faith, instinctive in the human mind,

upon which Jesus built. Taking the light which we all possess, he fans it into a divine blaze and re-lights our individual candles from the eternal fires of heaven. Surely no other person ever lived who did this as well as he. With a fresh simplicity, then, and a new earnestness, we should re-study the words of this inspired intellect, taking into account all their shadings, uncovering their subtle meanings, until the love of God and the law of good become the two dominant impulsions of our creative imagination. Patiently each should take himself by the hand and lead himself to the altar of a new faith through the exaltation of that Spirit which waits to blossom afresh in everyone's life.

The Master tells us that everyone who asks receives, that the door is opened when we knock, that we shall find what we seek. He also said that the gate through which we must enter is strait and the way narrow; that whatsoever things we would that men should do unto us we first must do unto them. We must reconcile these statements to the great law of cause and effect that Jesus taught, for he never departed from this law. For "this is the law and the prophets."

The gate to which he referred is the same gate that stood in front of the temple of Solomon, the gateway to the innermost sanctuary of our being, the Holy of Holies within us. In this Holy of Holies is the Ark of the Covenant, the spiritual Life Principle within us, and in this Ark is the Scroll of Life upon which is written the sacred word, the name of God, which is "I AM." "I AM" is a statement of pure and absolute being.

Entering this symbolic temple we must pass between two pillars, one representing law and order, the other love and feeling. They were called Jachin and Boaz, which means the personal and impersonal universe or our spontaneous use of impersonal laws. We can use these laws consciously. They must respond mechanically. The law of life responds to us by corresponding with our mental attitudes toward life.

If we would enter the sacred temple of our being our actions must be based on love, the great impulsion of life, and law, its great propulsion. Jesus balanced love and law—love, the givingness of the Divine Nature into blessing; law, the reaction to our thoughts and deeds automatically bringing a reward or punishment. We must so live that nothing which hurts can go from us. Then we shall knock on the right door. Then our hunger and thirst after righteousness will be filled, the door will be opened.

The treasure of life is already buried deep within our being. Seeking and finding, asking and receiving, giving and getting—this is the law of life. Jesus, the wayshower, the revealor of God, was an explorer of man's divinity. The two central themes of his teaching were love and the law, the personal and the impersonal, the Divine Spirit flowing through everything, incarnated in our own lives, and the automatic reaction of the law of cause and effect as justice without judgment, punishment without viciousness, and reward without partiality.

CHAPTER IV

Forgivingness

"THEN came Peter to him, and said, Lord, how oft shall my brother sin against me and I forgive him? Till seven times?" Jesus answered Peter by saying, "I say not unto thee until seven times, but until seventy times seven." There must be a continual state of forgiveness else there will be a continual state of unforgiveness.

And Jesus told them a parable explaining the meaning of forgiveness. He likened the Kingdom of God unto a king who, in looking over his accounts, discovered that one of his servants owed him a large sum of money. The king was about to foreclose on this obligation and sell the man and his wife and family into slavery for payment of the debt. But the servant besought him to have patience. So, moved with compassion, the king forgave him his debt.

If this were the whole story it would be incomplete for it implies a one-sided action between us and the universe. It implies that we can stand in front of a mirror without casting our reflection in it. It implies that we can take without giving. And this would not be just. Justice, the balance of action and equal reaction, would not be maintained. The law of cause and effect, which runs through everything, would be violated.

The servant who had been forgiven went out rejoicing. On his way he met one who owed him a small amount of money which he was unable to pay. The one who had been forgiven would not forgive, he would not wait until the obligation could be fulfilled. He cast the one who owed him into prison.

And now the compassion of Jesus passes into his sense of universal justice as he continues the parable of the unmerciful servant. It seems that friends of the one cast into prison came and told their lord what had been done. The recital of the lack of compassion of him who had been forgiven but who refused to forgive others caused the king to become angry. He commanded that the unmerciful servant be cast into prison until his own debt should be paid.

Jesus was the wisest man who ever lived, the most loving, the kindest and most compassionate. He was at the same time the most just. This story was an object lesson to teach that it is impossible to be forgiven unless we forgive. We cannot receive what we refuse to give. We cannot possess what we withhold. We cannot enter the gates of heaven unless we leave them open that others may enter. Too often we wish to receive without giving, to possess without sharing. This we can never do. It is only as we share the treasures of the Kingdom that we really possess them. Jesus, the master mind, had likened the law of cause and effect to the anger of a king who had the power to execute his will. He was not referring to an angry God.

On a certain day they brought to this man of compassion a woman taken in adultery, saying that according to the law of Moses she should be stoned. The Blessed One answered, "He that is without sin among you, let him first cast a stone at her." Convicted by their own conscience, they went out one by one, "from the eldest even unto the last," and Jesus was left alone with the woman.

Turning to her he asked, "Woman, where are those thine accusers? hath no man condemned thee?" "No man, Lord," she replied. And he answered, "Neither do I condemn thee: go, and sin no more." In forgiving the woman he told her to sin no more, for salvation is not *in* our mistakes but *from* them. Divine Forgivingness is not an excuse to continue in wrong action.

In no other act of Jesus was his love and understanding better shown than in this incident, recognized throughout Christian history as an outstanding example of the meaning of love. Should we not all follow his example and forgive ourselves and others? All have made mistakes and all need the release that comes from a consciousness of being forgiven.

Jesus, the incarnation of Cosmic Love, tells us to forgive not only once, or seven times, or seventy times, but seventy times seven. We must forgive until there is no longer anything that needs forgiveness. None of us can know when this time will come. But sometime, somewhere, the slate will be wiped clean.

The Great Physician used the law of life for healing the sick, the restoration of sanity and the betterment of circumstances. He multiplied loaves and fishes, fed the multitude, found money in a fish's mouth, and raised the dead. This was not done contrary to the law of life, but in accord with it. The only restriction he laid down for our conduct was that our desires shall conform to harmony, to love.

To desire that which is not life-giving is suicidal; to desire that which is life-giving is life more abundant. It was the more abundant life in conformity with good that Jesus advocated. He knew that we have freedom under law, that unity is not uniformity, that liberty is not license. If we desire evil for others, we shall bring it upon ourselves. While we would hurt another we can be hurt. This is justice and not the act of a vicious Deity. It is where action and reaction meet. A misuse of the law of cause and effect will finally so block and confuse our lives that we must start over again. This is why the Wise One coupled Divine Givingness with Divine Forgivingness.

Automatically the Divine Givingness forgives. The moment we cease using the law of cause and effect destructively we are freed from all previous misuse of it. Isaiah had caught a vision of this when he said, ". . . our sins (mistakes) shall be remembered no more against us forever." Though they were scarlet they shall become white as snow through the purification of Spirit.

According to Jesus we are not punished *for* our mistakes but *by* them. Therefore, we cannot be saved *in* our sins or mistakes. Salvation is *from* them and not in them. When we cease making the mistake, the punishment also ceases. This is the meaning of the story of the prodigal son and the parable of the man who came at the eleventh hour. This is why the great lover of God and man forgave the thief at the hour of his own crucifixion, saying, "Today shalt thou be with me in paradise."

What wonderful good would come to the world could we see this. Forgive and you shall be forgiven takes all harshness from the law of cause and effect and leaves each the arbiter of his own fate under that great law of justice without judgment that the most enlightened one was talking about. Jesus was the greatest judge who ever lived, but yet the only judge who passed no judgment on others.

"And, behold, they brought to him a man sick of the palsy." Perceiving their faith, he said to the sick man, "Son, be of good cheer; thy sins be forgiven thee." This was blasphemous to the scribes, but Jesus, knowing their thoughts, said, "Wherefore think ye evil in your hearts? For whether is easier, to say, Thy sins be forgiven thee; or to say, Arise, and walk? But that ye may know that the son of man hath power on earth to forgive sins, (then saith he to the sick of the palsy), Arise, take up thy bed, and go unto thine house."

It is now known that before the original flow of life can be restored any sense of guilt which obstructs this flow must be removed. Just as Jesus knew the thoughts of the scribes, he also knew the thoughts of the palsied man. He knew that he was suffering from a burden of guilt. The particular block which he removed was a subjective sense of self-condemnation. The man felt that he was rejected of life. It was this feeling that caused his disease.

It makes no difference whether we call this a body-mind relationship or a burden of the soul imposing itself on the body. The deep, penetrating love and compassion of the Man of Wisdom reached back to the place of innocence in the man, to a place which had never suffered condemnation, which was forever one with the Father.

Jesus, as was his habit, went immediately to the focal point of the disturbance. He told the man that his sins were forgiven him. He knew that all our troubles are tied back into, and spring from, a wrong relationship with the universe. Our inability to forgive others blocks us. Our inability to forgive ourselves provides an equal block and we cannot feel that we are forgiven until first we have forgiven others.

Always the Great Teacher deals with reality. How can we see the light for ourselves without taking others into that light? How can we receive without giving? How can anyone live exclusively if he belongs to a universe which is inclusive? How can one find God in himself without discovering God in others? "If the blind lead the blind, shall they not both fall into the ditch?"

We would so love to lay down our burdens and enter into a sanctuary of wholeness and peace. Before we can do this we must learn that the doorway to the Kingdom of God swings both ways. What we shut out shuts us out. Jesus winnows out the last shred of self-conceit. This makes his teaching difficult to follow. It is well enough to say that we love God, that we would follow Christ, that we seek full salvation. This is but a natural desire for self-preservation. But do we realize that the light that flows through heaven's gate flows both ways and excludes none?

Jesus was no merely soft spoken teacher. His love was so great that he did not hesitate to teach the law of that love. God will not and cannot change His nature to suit our whimsical fancy or bigotry or self-conceit. Justice, like love and mercy, flows. We cannot enter this stream without flowing along with it.

It is not easy to follow the example of one who had so perfectly balanced love and law. We want what we want when we want it and in the way we want it. But are we willing to believe that a law that can bring us what we want when we want it must inevitably return to us what we send out in it?

The idea of Divine Love is so wonderful that we yearn toward it with irresistible desire. We need it as we need no other thing on earth or in heaven. We would enter into its protection, its security and peace. Jesus tells us that if we would experience this love we must remain true to its nature. If we would enter into wholeness we must give up that which is un-whole.

In saying that "no man putteth a piece of new cloth unto an old garment" and "neither do men put new wine into old bottles," he points to one of the subtle mysteries of our mental and spiritual lives. The most effective way to displace a negative emotion is to find a positive one which absorbs it. Thus hate is swallowed up by love and fear dies when enveloped in faith.

What untold misery would be redeemed if we would use the transforming power of love to heal hate, the radiance of joy to overcome despair. But we cannot serve both God and mammon. We cannot attach hate to love nor disturb peace with the discord of confusion. We must forsake the one if we would enter into the other.

Jesus, the unparalleled character of history, penetrated the depth, and beyond, of modern Science of Mind. The psychic pathway must be cleared from our adult experience back to the innocence of the infant. All blocks must be removed that the original flow of spontaneous life may resume its course. He knew better than modern research has discovered that while we entertain anything which contradicts our union with God we shall suffer. Not because God imposes this suffering, but because our own act interferes with the nature of our being. It is only when nature and act become one that there is a complete clearance from the Universal Soul into the individual life.

No greater comfort can be found in all the teachings of Jesus than in his concept of the possibility of finding heaven here and now. We all have a sense of condemnation, which at times is so great that it seems impossible to feel our way back to God. The hope and assurance which the Wayshower gave enables us to find release, not in some theoretical future but in the eternal here-and-now in which he consciously lived. Always today is the day of salvation—this day which extends from eternity to eternity but which is always focussed in the present moment.

This was one of the fundamental teachings of this great spiritual genius. We should look upon it as a principle in nature and our relationship with God. Nothing in the universe holds anything against us. Nothing vindictive can flow from the Spirit. When we turn to It, trusting and believing, the avenues of Its outpush through us are unlocked. That life which is eternally new and fresh flows into us as water gushing from the hidden spring of our being. We must drink of this water. God has given us the cup of life which must be used as a chalice of love. The stream flows around and through us, but the Spirit cannot drink for us.

Jesus knew the frailties of the human mind. Above and beyond these frailties he knew a Divine Power and a loving Presence whose whole nature is to bless —the God of love who does not condemn. Would it be too much to say that he taught that there is no sin but a mistake and no punishment but a consequence?

And so the Master walked and talked, lived and

loved. And one day, being wearied, he came to Jacob's well and while he sat there a woman of Samaria came to draw water. "Jesus saith unto her, Give me to drink." The woman replied by inquiring how he, a Jew, could ask water from a woman of Samaria. He answered by telling her that just as physical water quenches physical thirst, so there is a spiritual water within us from which, if we drink, we shall never thirst again; that whoever drinks of this water will discover within himself "a well of water springing up into everlasting life."

There is a perennial spring of life gushing from the rock of our being. It was this rock that Moses struck with his staff of truth. But the individual stream soon dries up unless it is kept open to the ocean of life. The only conditions Jesus laid down for keeping this stream open were that we live, love and rejoice, recognize the source within and around us, imbibe its spirit, incarnate its grace, enter into it and leave the door open that all others may enter.

And the Great One added: You cannot carry grief to the well of joy if you would drink happiness. You cannot carry hurt to the mountain of vision. You cannot carry disunity to the undivided Kingdom of Goodness if you would enter in. You cannot lay hate upon the altar of faith if you would find love. This simple teaching is self-evident. It is its simplicity that eludes us. Who would not drink of the water of everlasting life and enter into the joy of the Kingdom of Good? Indeed, this has been the struggle of humanity since time began.

After telling the woman at the well that each has a well-spring of living water within himself, Jesus next explained the meaning of true worship: "God is spirit, and every one who worships him must worship him in spirit and in truth." This implies a universal Spirit equally distributed, everywhere present, and available to all.

It is because God is present everywhere and is the source of all being that He is at the center of our own individual lives. It is this center of being, this source of life, to which Jesus referred when he told the woman that he had "meat to eat that ye know not of," that holding communion with this Spirit we drink the waters of life and eat the bread of life.

"The Father seeketh such." There is a gentle but persistent pressure back of our thoughts and acts seeking to guide us to the fountain of life. There is not only a daily communion with the Spirit that we need, but also a daily renewal of our mental and physical being through the indrawing of spiritual essence, which is the ultimate substance of all things.

Physical eating and drinking is symbolic of an equal necessity that corresponds to it—the need that the mind shall partake of that Divine Substance which is the bread of life and drink from that Divine

Fountain which is the water of life. To drink only from the physical fountain and eat material bread alone is not enough. The meal is not complete until we have discovered that substance of Spirit, that essence of Reality which underlies everything. This is why the Illumined One said that we cannot live by bread alone but by every word that proceedeth out of the mouth of God.

Somewhere along the line we shall be called upon to surrender the lesser to a greater Self, to surrender all sense of isolated salvation to that all-inclusive beneficence which causes its rain and sun to come alike on the just and the unjust. God grant that this day shall be the one in which we are living.

CHAPTER V

The Human Family

MODERN knowledge coincides with the teaching of Jesus that we must first cast the beam out of our own eye if we would help our fellowman. It is now known that an emotional bias can create an intellectual blind spot, making it impossible to judge correctly when there is prejudice.

In an ordinary analysis, if the physician has certain blocks within himself that correspond with identical ones in his patient's mind, it will be difficult, if not impossible, for the physician to get through the block in his patient. If the physician had unconsciously disliked his own father it would be difficult for him to proceed with the analysis of a patient who likewise had disliked his father. The analysis would stop at this point and proceed no further until the block had been removed. It is accepted that before one is equipped to practice analytical psychology he must have gotten rid of the emotional blocks in his own consciousness, otherwise they will either project themselves in to his patient or become a hindrance to the analysis.

The profound understanding of these facts which Jesus possessed nearly two thousand years before modern methods of investigation uncovered them, is proof enough that he had spiritual clairvoyance. There is nothing in the mind of man which was hidden to him. "If the blind lead the blind, shall they not both fall into the ditch?" There must be a seeing eye. How can we heal someone of sadness if we ourselves are sad? How can we generate faith in others unless we first have faith? How can we extend a refreshing draught with an empty cup? "Physician, heal thyself" should be the keynote for our desire to help others. Only the guided can guide.

We are hypocrites if we try to give what we do not possess. This calls for a terrific soul-searching, a complete inward healing. By the same token, wherever we have first healed ourselves we shall be able to help others. If we are free from the blight of fear we can help others to a place of faith. If our whole consciousness responds to love our presence automatically will heal hate.

In one of his parables the Great Teacher likened the Kingdom of Heaven to ten virgins who took their lamps and went forth to meet the bridegroom. Five of these virgins were wise and five foolish. The foolish ones took their lamps but no oil, while the wise ones provided oil for their lamps. In the middle of the night when the bridegroom came all arose and trimmed their lamps, but the foolish ones said to the wise, "Give us of your oil, for our lamps have gone out."

Continuing this same thought Jesus likened the Kingdom of Heaven to a man who gave a certain number of talents to each of his servants, after which he departed. Some multiplied their talents while some hid theirs in the ground. After a time the lord returned and sought an accounting from his servants. Those who had increased the talents he had loaned them were commended while those who had hid theirs away and not used them were condemned as unprofitable.

The talents we possess can be multiplied only through use. The wise virgins were those whose wicks ran deep in the oil of Spirit. The oil of love is always flowing but there must be a place in us where the intake and outgo are equal. To receive without giving is congestion and stagnation. To give without receiving produces inertia and exhaustion.

Just as there must be an intake or there can be no outgo, so there must be an outgo or there can be no intake. If we bury the talent it remains static, inactive, unproductive. We must use or temporarily lose (there can be no eternal loss). That which we refuse to multiply we lose the use of. That which we refuse to give cannot come back multiplied. It is only when the divine circulation is permitted to flow in an uninterrupted stream that the giving and taking can equalize.

In the parable of the talents we find one of those hard sayings in the teaching of Jesus which so easily could be misunderstood. For he said that the man who refused to use his talents, like the foolish virgin who refused to keep her lamp trimmed and burning, lost even the little he had.

In the long run everyone who loves is loved. All who give joy receive it back. Everything moves in circles, in cycles of cause and effect. More is added to the much we use. When we refuse to use our gifts they shrivel up. The divine flow is shortcircuited. The one who gives for the joy of giving will receive back even more joy than he gave out. Ever as the volume increases the circle will increase. There can be no point of saturation in that which is infinite.

"For whosoever hath, to him shall be given, and he shall have more abundance: but whosoever hath not, from him shall be taken away even that he hath." Jesus taught the two great fundamental realities of being—love and law. It would have been impossible for him to avoid teaching the exactness of the law of cause and effect. It was necessary for him to show that even though God is infinite love, the universe is governed by immutable law.

With this in mind let us seek to discover what the Master meant when he said that those who have shall receive more while those who have not shall lose what they possess. If one has friendship in his heart, shall not such a one have friends? Surely to him will be given. Friends will come from the corners of the earth to sit in his presence. In his wholeness they will find their own wholeness.

Who finds God in man will also find man in God. Such a one cannot walk alone but feels divine companionship with the simplest soul, the communion of like with like. Not only does this apply in the greatest of all gifts, which is love, it applies with equal force to all human relationships. The one who has a consciousness of joy will meet joy. The one who sings will hear a song. The one who turns from evil will find good. He will be as one divinely guided and guarded by the Spirit Itself.

This is the meaning of many of the parables of Jesus—simple, beautiful and profound. The invitation to surrender our weakness to the power of Spirit, our littleness to Its greatness, that we be not lost but found. True submission is not to a greater force but to a higher intelligence. It is the letting go of everything that denies the Kingdom of God and the laying hold of those things whch affirm its presence here and now. The day of God's appointing is not tomorrow. It is in the breath we breathe in this present moment as we turn to that which knows only the joy of its own being. The action of the Spirit on our consciousness and our consciousness, through law, on our environment, is real, dynamic and creative.

And he spoke to them in another parable, saying, "Behold, a sower went forth to sow." Some seeds fell by the way, some upon stony places, some among thorns, while others fell into fertile soil. The seed which fell into fertile soil brought forth fruit, it was multiplied a hundred fold. While Jesus usually made no attempt to explain his teaching but sometimes said, "Who hath ears to hear, let him hear," on this occasion he did explain the meaning of the parable.

He told them that the seed is the word. He likened the mind to the creative soil into which a seed falls. If it falls on stony ground it cannot take deep root. When trouble comes it is easily uprooted, it endures but for a short time.

He likened the seed which fell among thorns to those who hear the word of truth but are so confused by other thoughts that the word cannot bear fruit. But he said that the seed which falls into deep, rich soil is like the word which draws life from the eternal source of all being. This is the word that increases and multiplies. This is the word of power.

In another parable of a sower Jesus spoke of one who sowed good seed in his field while his enemies came and sowed tares among the wheat. He said that when the time of harvest comes the tares will be gathered together and burned while the wheat will be gathered into the barns. Finally evil will be swallowed up in good; in the all-consuming fires of experience the dross and slag must be cast out that the good alone may remain.

This process is going on within all of us and will continue until the final triumph of Spirit. This triumph is inevitable, but the day of its coming is not appointed. That day lies in man's choice. It may be today or it may run into innumerable tomorrows as each day casts its shadow down the pathway even to evening time and night. But as night lengthens into a new dawn the sun again rises, renewing hope and prophesying triumph.

The scribes and Pharisees, who so carefully observed external rites, took Jesus to task, saying that his disciples transgressed the tradition of the elders because they did not wash their hands before eating. The answer of the Man of Wisdom was consistent with his entire philosophy of life: "This people draweth nigh unto me with their mouth, and honoreth me with their lips: but their heart is far from me."

Turning to the multitude he said, "Not that which goeth into the mouth defileth a man; but that which cometh out of the mouth, this defileth him." It is not alone the external act that is important, for, as the Great Master said, it is out of the heart that evil proceeds. This is what really defiles a person. To the pure all is pure.

In explaining this teaching Paul said, "I know and am persuaded by the Lord Jesus that there is nothing unclean of itself but to him that esteemeth anything to be unclean, to him it is unclean." In the study of mental conflicts it has been discovered that they arise when the mind is divided against itself; when we permit ourselves to do things, consciously or unconsciously, which, consciously or unconsciously, we condemn ourselves for doing. Paul understood the nature of this conflict and said it can be resolved only through love which conquers fear, dissolves hate and sets us on the pathway of life surrounded by the full armor of faith, which is light.

"Hast thou faith? have it to thyself before God. Happy is he that condemneth not himself in that thing which he alloweth." If this were understood and incorporated in our lives our conflicts would disappear. We are happy when life flows through us into creative self-expression. This cannot happen while we judge ourselves or others. When we so live that nothing goes from us but love there will be no condemnation of ourselves or others.

Every man's world is in his own mind. Every man's kingdom is in his own heart. Every man's relationship to life is in his own consciousness. The external act, to be pure, must flow from an inward fountain of purity. Those who have failed to purify their own souls cannot possibly purify others. This, Jesus said, would be the blind leading the blind. It is only where there is an inner spiritual awareness that there can be a seeing eye or a true divine guidance. There is no possible camouflage in truth. We may fool ourselves and others; we cannot fool the Spirit or the law of cause and effect.

Paul also said, "For though I preach the gospel, I have nothing to glory of: for necessity is laid upon me; yea, woe is unto me, if I preach not the gospel!" Everyone must live according to his convictions. One who has spiritual convictions and refuses to live by them is a house divided against itself. It is when we live up to the light we have that we can expect more light. When we receive the light, not so much a duty as an impulsion is laid upon us to live by that light. To refuse to live by the spiritual light we have is temporarily to cut off the source of more light which we all desire. The Apostle tells us that we will be humble in this when we realize the light is not from ourselves but from the Lord.

The writings of Paul show that he not only had a deep appreciation of spiritual things, he also understood the laws of our psychic life. In many places the Bible implies that as we have a physical and a spiritual life, so we also have a psychic life. Whether we wish to call this the collective unconscious, the race mind, the carnal mind, or think of it as the law of mind in action, makes no difference. It is referred to in many places in the Bible. It is the "sea" which Moses parted; the waters engulfing the earth described in the story of The Flood; the sea into which Jonah fell. It was this sea over which the Ark, the vehicle of the spiritual life, floated. It was this sea over which Jesus walked and whose tempests he stilled. And we find a reference to it in Revelation where it says, "And there shall be no more sea."

There would not be so many references to the sea in the greatest book of wisdom ever written unless they had a deep meaning. The sea definitely has reference to something we must expect to find in ourselves, in all humanity, and in nature itself. The Bible begins its story with the assumption that man is spirit, soul and body. His body is one with all physical creation, his spirit one with God, while his soul is his subjective life. We call this his subconscious or unconscious mind, the repository of all his thoughts and emotions acting as an impersonal law in his life.

All our thoughts, feelings and emotions find a permanent center within, from which they react upon our physical bodies and our physical environments. They control us until we control them. If we add the subjective reactions of all individual lives together, we arrive at what has been called the collective unconscious and what the Bible calls the carnal mind which is enmity to God. This really means the law of mind in action, both individually and collectively.

In this collective mind are laid down the thoughts and beliefs which the whole race has accepted, acting as a law of human conduct and influencing everyone. The whole psychic or subjective atmosphere of the race has been called "the sea." Moses, with his rod of truth, representing the authority of God, was able to divide the waters of the psychic life, symbolized by the Red Sea, and pass through to the shores of spiritual realization, carrying with him the children of the "I AM," those who understood their relationship with the one and only God.

The law of mind in action, wrongly used by the collective group, brings confusion upon the whole earth, just as it does in the individual life. Moses had power to *part* these psychic waters. It was left to the supreme spiritual wisdom of Jesus to walk *over* them, to still the waves and the storms of the psychic life. When in Revelation it says there shall be no more sea, it refers to that time when the entire race confusion shall have been done away with through a knowledge of our unity with God.

This can be brought about only by mutual consent and right action. This does not mean that we should all think or act alike, for each is a unique center in the one Mind, each is an individual in the one Life. But it is impossible to get back to our original source without first overcoming those psychological reactions which not only deny this original source but which act contrary to it.

Paul understood these things and referred to them when he said, ". . . I would not that ye should be ignorant, how that all our fathers . . . passed through the sea . . . and did all eat the same spiritual meat; And did all drink the same spiritual drink: for they drank of that spiritual Rock . . . and that Rock was Christ." As in the re-orientation of the individual life it is necessary to penetrate all psychic confusion that the mind may be re-integrated, so the Bible implies that there is a world psychic life which must be controlled by bringing everyone back to the Rock of Christ.

Paul says that those who fail to find this Christ are still lost in the wilderness. In the Old Testament we find that they were submerged by the sea. He says that they were "destroyed of the destroyer."

This "destroyer" is not God, who is life, but a misuse of the laws of life, which, wrongly used, become the destroyer until Christ brings them under control. In light of our knowledge of the relationship of the mind to the body and our thinking to our environment, it should not seem strange that there could be a collective mind, the thoughts of the whole race, which largely controls us.

Watching the lives of those who have to some degree mastered their thoughts we can imagine what would happen if the majority of the race should do so. War, poverty and human indignity would cease. We do not know when this will be brought about but all human evolution is moving toward this divine event. We have already reached a point where we are subduing physical laws to individual and collective purposes and the next great endeavor will be in the realm of mind and spirit.

This psychic redemption of humanity is not to be laughed off. There are physical laws, psychical laws and spiritual laws. It is only when the physical and pschological are brought under control of the spiritual that the Kingdom of Heaven can come on earth. That divine event which the wise have prophesied, the poets written about and the hope of man reached toward, is not an illusion. It is the greatest of all possibilities, the highest of all realities.

There should be no sense of mystery about this.

We need not become lost in occult or esoteric symbolism but find the real milk and meat of its meaning. We shall discover it in a few simple facts, thoughts and ideas. We live in a physical, mental and spiritual universe simultaneously. The three are, or ought to become, one. When we are governed by the Spirit our psychological reactions will become spiritualized, and, in their turn, dominate the physical. Whether we realize it or not we are on the pathway of this kind of evolution. Every great religion ever given to the world is some revelation leading toward the final consummation, the complete triumph of Spirit.

A certain young man came to Jesus and calling him "Good Master," asked, " . . . what shall I do to have eternal life?" Perhaps the young man was surprised at the answer: "Why callest thou me good? There is none good but one, that is God." This shows that Jesus never expected us to worship him either as a person or a God. He pointed to the one supreme Presence as the sole and only object of deific adoration. "There is none good save one, that is God." He told the young man to worship God alone, and added, "If thou wilt enter into life, keep the commandments."

The Supreme Teacher did not say, if you will enter into salvation or immortality, but "if thou wilt enter into *life,*" you will have to obey the rules of living. These rules he had already summed up in his teaching of the Fatherhood of God and the brotherhood of man and the necessity of a childlike trust and faith. These are the rules of the game of life—doing unto others as we would like them to do unto us, and doing it first; tolerance and kindness, understanding and compassion, sympathy and helpfulness, forgiving even as we would like to be forgiven.

Jesus placed no emphasis on theology or dogmas; his emphasis was on our relationship to life and to each other. He told the young man that if he wished to get the most out of living he would have to follow these rules.

Now this young man had great wealth and Jesus, being able to read people's thought, knew that he placed more emphasis on his wealth than he did on the Kingdom of Heaven. His wealth seemed more tangible to him than the Kingdom, therefore it was a block to his mind. So the Master tested the young man with this proposition: would he be willing to forsake his wealth? Jesus did not condemn the wealth. What he was trying to illustrate was that we sometimes have to lose our lives to find them. Where the treasure is, there is the heart also.

The young man had already told him that he had followed the laws of Moses since his youth. He had lived an exemplary life. To Jesus this was not enough. Merely to be moral and ethical is not enough. This young man had not made a complete surrender to the Spirit although he had observed the laws of Moses. He was good, he was honest, he was upright, but in a negative way. Seeing the block to his complete surrender, the Wise One asked if he could give up everything and follow the Truth wherever it might lead. This the young man could not bring himself to do, nor can many of us. Jesus had made this surrender and he knew that no one ever makes it without discovering a new country, a new hope, a larger life.

And he spoke to them in a parable about laborers. There was a certain man who had a vineyard. Early in the morning he hired laborers to work for a penny a day. Later in the day he hired other men, at the third, the sixth and the eleventh hour, and when evening came he called them all together and each received the same compensation. Naturally, many objected to this, but the lord of the vineyard said, " . . . I will give unto this last, even as unto thee." I will do "what I will with mine own. Is thine eye evil, because I am good?"

In this parable Jesus was likening the vineyard to life and the laborers to our relationship with it. Those who early in their experience come to understand their relationship to the lord of the vineyard, and those who discover the laws of life later in the day, must all finally reap the same reward. In other words, God gives as fast as we can receive. God and the spiritual kingdom are timeless. There is no late and no early in the Divine Mind.

Solomon with all his wisdom knew nothing about electricity, therefore he was compelled to use a candle. God had not withheld anything from him, for God had already given him all he could take. Thousands of years later someone discovered electricity, coming in at the eleventh hour, as it were. God was not partial to the one who later discovered electricity. He merely gave him what he could take. To those who accused the lord of the vineyard of being partial his answer was, "Is thine eye evil because I am good?" Have you less because others possess a good equal to yours? Is there not good enough to go around?

All do not learn the laws of life and the rules of the game of living in the same hour. Is it wrong that we should have the benefits of electricity because Solomon and Moses knew nothing about them? Are the comforts of modern invention evil because antiquity did not enjoy them? The great lesson is that life delivers itself into our capacity to receive it. The outpouring from the cosmic horn of plenty can only fill the cup that is lifted up toward it. A pail turned on its side cannot be filled with rain from heaven.

The lord of the vineyard stands for the love of God and the givingness of the Spirit. The vineyard represents the fruits of life. We are the laborers, and the reward, the compensation, is the law of cause and effect which measures to each according to his acts. The ones who came in at an earlier hour represent those who have gained some slight knowledge of spiritual things before others. They are indeed fortunate. But the ones who came in at the third, the sixth and the eleventh hours also entered into the Kingdom and their reward must be equal to those who came first.

If yesterday we did not know that God is love, then yesterday we could not enter into communion with that love. If we do not discover this until late in the afternoon of tomorrow, then we may know that all the yesterdays of fear and hurt will vanish. In the hour of recognition love comes full-orbed into our present experience. This parable is a lesson of hope. We are all searching, we are on the pathway of self-discovery. This self-discovery cannot be separated from the discovery of God, for God is the supreme Self, the everpresent Reality. We have always been living in the divine sea of life but we have not realized it. The awakening is not to God but to man.

One morning when Jesus and his disciples were returning to the city they passed a fig tree which had no fruit "but leaves only." And Jesus said, "Let no fruit grow on that henceforth forever." The fig tree withered away so quickly that the disciples marveled. This is one of the few, and perhaps the only, incident in the life of the Blessed One where he used his tremendous power in this manner. Possibly he was using the fig tree as an example of what negative thought can do, because it was an inanimate object. Possibly he chose it merely as a way of showing that even nature responds to man's thought for good or for ill. It certainly amazed the disciples for they murmured among themselves, saying, "How soon is the fig tree withered away!"

One lesson we can learn from this is that we should bless rather than curse, that all negative thought has some influence in ourselves and on our environment. Our attitude toward life should be affirmative, life-giving, up-building. Should we watch our thinking for a day would we not be surprised to learn how many times in a few hours we are cursing our environment, our bodies, the things we are doing or the people around us? Not cursing them consciously, of course, so much as thinking about them negatively. Do we not say, "My poor head!" "My poor feet!" "My unfortunate circumstances!" "My misunderstandings with people!"?

Let us remember the incident of the fig tree and not permit our thoughts to wither up our experiences, to make them unproductive, unfruitful. Surely we should bless everything, thinking of everything from the standpoint of increase, of goodness, of truth and of beauty.

This simple practice alone could convert our consciousness and transform our environment. The only effort it would take would be the self-discipline of thought control and our emotional reactions to life. The best way to arrive at this affirmative attitude toward life would be to realize that there is spiritual substance and presence in everything, that God reveals Himself through all nature, that the Universal Soul looks through all eyes and feels the joy of its own living in all our activities. If we were firmly convinced that this is true would we not always be seeking to uncover the Divinity in everything, through praise, through blessing and through thanksgiving?

The response of Jesus to the disciples' wonder was, "Verily I say unto you, if ye have faith and doubt not, ye shall not only do this which is done to the fig tree, but also if ye shall say unto this mountain, Be thou removed, and be thou cast into the sea, it shall be done. And all things whatsoever ye shall ask in prayer, believing, ye shall receive."

Whether we think the mountain to which he referred was symbolic or literal makes no difference. He may have been referring to any obstruction in the pathway of spiritual progress. " . . . whatsoever ye shall ask in prayer, believing, ye shall receive."

This "whatsoever" must include everything—all the experiences that make up our everyday living, everything that we contact and all people we meet. Whatsoever includes both great and small.

Jesus praised those who had multiplied their gifts and condemned those who had held them so tightly that no law of increase could follow, saying that those who had been faithful over a little would be given authority over much. And again he says that to those who have shall be given and from those who have not shall be taken away.

If we tend the small garden of our present experience, planting it in love, cultivating it with patience, and being willing to divide the harvest with others, we shall discover a law of increase which tends to multiply the good we now possess. Carefully nurturing and cultivating such faith as we have, such kindness and peace as we possess, we find life not only giving back to us the original type of our planting, but multiplying it in every direction.

This Jesus illustrates in the parable of the ten pieces of money which he used as a symbol of the divine gifts that God has imparted to us. Through using these gifts we multiply them; otherwise, they tend to diminish so that even the little good we have withers in the hand which holds it too tightly. This is the way of life, nor can all the wit of man change it.

Perhaps we have waited for some great occasion, some spectacular event, when with heroic resolve we shall proclaim the Kingdom of God. And having waited, nothing has happened, while the days gather themselves into the years and the years die and hope vanishes and faith sinks into despair. We have failed to realize that the unplanted seed can never grow, the unused talent can never multiply.

The Great Revelator proclaims the eternal day, the everlasting hour, that minute of time compressed from eternity and expanding again into eternity. Now is the day of salvation. The harvest is ripe today. There is no future to us other than that which presses itself forth from our present. There is no past other than our memories. Too often we limit the present by the past and the future by the present. While Jesus tells us that our lives should expand in every direction; life is to be lived, beauty enjoyed, love expressed. A song must be sung.

At the Feast of the Passover, the Last Supper, that symbolic occasion when Jesus "laid aside his garments and took a towel and girded himself" and began to wash the disciples' feet, the tempestuous Peter "said unto him, Thou shalt never wash my feet." The answer was: "If I wash thee not, thou hast no part with me." This lesson of washing the disciples' feet probably has two meanings. Its outward meaning is one of humility and brotherly love.

Its inward meaning probably came down from an ancient ritual based on the idea that nature serves us when we first obey it.

Jesus, the Lord and Master, represented the law of life which must be understood and obeyed before it can be used. Therefore, he answers Peter's remonstrance by saying, "If I wash thee not, thou hast no part with me." It is only as there is a complete unity between God and man, between the Master and the servant, between the laws of nature and our conscious use of them, that definite results can follow.

When Jesus explained this to Peter, Peter exclaimed, "Lord, not my feet only, but also my hands and my head." The Master answered by saying, "He that is washed needeth not save to wash his feet." In ancient symbolism "feet" were considered the tie between heaven and earth, where heaven and earth join, the union of heaven and earth. Therefore, the feet only need to be washed. That which is of heaven is already clean.

This was undoubtedly the hidden meaning of washing the disciples' feet, but its practical application is one of union and humility, one of brotherly love and mutual helpfulness, for, as Jesus said, "If I, then, your lord and master, have washed your feet, ye ought also to wash one another's feet . . . For I have given you an example that ye should do as I have done to you."

It is impossible to study the words of the Way-shower without realizing that his whole teaching was a symbolic presentation of our relationship to the universe. He was the great example and not the great exception, therefore he said, "I do this as an example unto you." And he added, "If ye know these things, happy are you if ye do them." It is useless to have knowledge unless we use it. Jesus taught the exact parallel between the physical laws of nature and the laws of mind in relationship to the spiritual world. The key to his teaching is an understanding that for every physical law there is a parallel law in mind and spirit.

As there is a law of attraction and repulsion in physics, so there is a mental law of attraction and repulsion. As there are physical energies, so there are spiritual energies. One does not contradict the other, for the spiritual includes the mental and the physical. As the laws of nature serve us when we first obey them, so spiritual powers minister to us when we obey spiritual laws. As all energies in nature converge in one ultimate energy, so all individual minds and spirits have a common Mind and Spirit, which is God.

And the Master asked his disciples, "What would ye that I should do for you?" The disciples, being human, answered, "Grant unto us that we may sit one on thy right hand and the other on thy left hand in thy glory." How human we all are! Who would not sit at the right hand of Christ in celestial glory? In his answer Jesus showed a patience which was one of his outstanding qualities. He asked if they could drink of the cup that he drank from or be baptized with the same baptism, and said, "And whosoever of you shall be the chiefest, shall be the servant of all."

The Universal Soul cannot exclude anyone from Its warm embrace. But we cannot be conscious of that embrace while we refuse it to others. Jesus taught the Fatherhood of God and the brotherhood of man. This Fatherhood cannot be realized unless and until it includes the brotherhood. In our stupidity we like to include the Fatherhood for ourselves only. We like to be right among all men. We like to feel that our method is the only correct one. But Reality will be accepted on its own terms alone.

These terms include the necessity that we see all humanity on the pathway of one divine and certain destiny; that we be willing to walk along with others, helping and being helped, loving and being loved, giving and being given to, until finally through love and compassion for each other we find that greater love which is the givingness of Life to all who receive it. "To as many as believed, gave he the power."

CHAPTER VI

The Kingdom

"COME, ye blessed of my Father, inherit the kingdom prepared for you from the foundation of the world." What a wonderful invitation to enter into the more complete life! Like other great spiritual teachers, Jesus believed in eternal verities which never change. He believed in a heavenly Kingdom forever established in the Mind of God, a Kingdom which all men ultimately must enter. Unlike most, he did not delay entering into this Kingdom until some future date. He said that it is to be entered into now, for it is at hand.

Reducing the teaching of Jesus to its utmost simplicity we find the central theme of his thought was that there is a spiritual prototype or pattern in the Mind of God which is the true cause and equivalent of our physical universe. Man is a spiritual being now, he is an immortal soul now as much as he ever can become, he already *is* a spirit, he lives in God now, and the nature of God flows through him at this moment. Man has already inherited the Kingdom of God. This Kingdom was prepared from the foundation of the world. It already exists. It waits our recognition.

It was the habit of Jesus to impart his great teaching through the use of familiar illustrations which all can understand. And so he asked his disciples if they were to go to a friend's home at midnight and ask for bread, would he turn them away by saying, "The door is shut and I cannot take time to give to you"? Would not that friend rise and give them as many loaves as they had need of? "And I say unto you, Ask and it shall be given you; seek, and ye shall find; knock, and it shall be opened unto you."

The universal Spirit never refuses anyone's approach. The doorway of God's Kingdom is opened to all who knock. The bread of life is given to all who ask. The power to live is imparted to all who will receive it. The message of Jesus includes every race, every creed, every doctrine, all groups of people, then and now. It includes you and me, today, just as much as it did his immediate followers.

Have we really knocked at the doorway of the larger life? Have we asked for that divine bread which comes from heaven, that wine made from the grapes of love, that divine guidance which can lead us in the right path? The great Man of God said that everyone who asks receives; that the door is opened to all who knock; that the bread and wine of life are given to all who hunger and thirst after righteousness.

And now he makes this teaching even more explicit by saying that if we ask for bread we shall not receive a stone. If we ask for a fish we shall not receive a serpent. If we ask for an egg we shall not receive a scorpion. We should not explain this away as though it were only a symbol of spiritual gifts. For Jesus used the actual figures of a loaf of bread, an egg and a fish. He is telling us how our daily needs may be met as they arise; that life does not withhold even the simplest thing from us. We are to enjoy life to the fullest.

He likens the Kingdom of God to a small grain of mustard seed, which, permitted to grow, becomes a great herb so that the birds of the air may lodge in its branches. He is telling us that even out of the small beginnings in our experiment with faith there shall surely grow a shelter of protection. The great Tree of Life will spread its branches over us. What hope and comfort we should take from this! What courage should come to us when we realize that there is a law of growth in the expansion of consciousness and if we persist we shall finally attain!

Again the Great Teacher likens the Kingdom to leaven hid in meal until the whole lump becomes leavened. The leaven is the yeast of faith, the permeation of consciousness with the seed of hope, of trust and of love. This is the bread of life which comes down from heaven. Perhaps the yeast can be likened to that divine impulsion which God has implanted in us and which cannot be taken away. Even all our mistakes cannot obliterate it. Some day the leaven will work, the whole lump will rise, the bread of life will be eaten and we shall no longer be hungry.

And Jesus likened the Kingdom of Heaven to a a treasure hid in a field which a man found and for the joy of its possession sold all he had in order that he might purchase the field. Those great souls who have discovered the Kingdom of God hid in their own consciousness have been glad to leave everything else. It is losing one's life to find it. The treasure of love, of life and of hope, the treasure of faith and confidence—who would not sell all else to possess them?

Yet, this treasure is already hidden in the innermost center of our being. God hid it there but God cannot discover it for us, for God cannot discover what He already knows. It is man who must discover the treasure, the Kingdom and the Spirit. A consciousness of this Kingdom is within everyone. There is within us a divine impatience, an intuitive yearning, an intellectual inquisitiveness that will not let us rest until we go in search for Reality, and, searching, find.

Again the Master likened the Kingdom to a pearl of great price, the central jewel in a crown of perfection. Gladly did the merchant who saw it sell all that he had that he might possess this marvelous jewel which shone forth in its purity. It was a wise merchant who discovered this pearl, a wiser one who recognized it, and the wisest of all who kept it.

Jesus said that those who discover the Kingdom are like ones who bring treasures from new things and from old. That is, in seeking new truth we should not forget what was good in the old. Truth never takes anything from us but adds to what we have.

And this spiritual genius likens the Kingdom of Heaven to a man who prepared a marriage feast for his son and invited his freinds. But they were too busy to come. One went to his farm, another to his merchandise. This so angered the king that he destroyed them and told his servants to go out into the highways and byways and gather together everyone they could find, both good and bad, that they might partake of the feast, saying that they were more worthy than the others. Isaiah had prophesied this day when he said, "Everyone who thirsteth come to the fountain and drink. And whosoever will may come."

Jesus was speaking about our willingness to receive the Kingdom. Most of us are too busy with other things—not that there is anything wrong with these other things, but when they occupy our attention to the exclusion of the Kingdom they must be destroyed. This is why he said that the king "destroyed those murderers and burned up their city."

We should not interpret this as having anything to do with a concept of hell and eternal damnation. Jesus was not a crude person but he did know that sooner or later right alone must reign. Back of this parable there is a philosophy which interprets the rise and fall of empire, the budding, blossoming and decay of civilization after civilization. Whenever any individual, group, nation or civilization, consciously or unconsciously, complies with the Divine Nature it will prosper, and whenever it no longer complies its possessions will be laid waste. The cycle must start over again to the end that somehow, somewhere, sometime, the thing shall be done rightly, in league with the Divine Will, which is the Divine Nature.

In the same parable we are told that the king, coming to the feast, saw one man who had not put on a wedding garment and commanded his servants to "bind him hand and foot" and take him away. As in much oriental literature, the wedding feast means the marriage of a servant to her lord, the union of man with God. The wedding garment is the seamless robe of unity. It is made of one piece, undivided and indivisible. It was this robe that Jesus wore. Therefore, we should interpret this part of the parable as meaning that we can partake of the wedding feast only when we don the wedding garment, only when we become aware of our unity with God.

And Jesus tells us that the old garment must be thrown into the fire. This expression has confused many: "Cast him into utter darkness. There shall be weeping and gnashing of teeth, for many are called but few are chosen." We should interpret this in the light of his whole teaching and with an understanding of oriental word pictures. The "utter darkness" has also been called "the dark night of the soul," that state of mind which finds itself isolated from the eternal light. The "weeping and gnashing of teeth" which follows is the anguish of the mind seeking to regain its lost paradise.

But who can doubt that in the divine plan every soul shall find its way; that the light of God, like His love, shall penetrate this outer darkness, flooding it with divine effulgence? It is our ignorance that needs enlightening. While we remain in this ignorance we remain in darkness.

But there is a divine ray that penetrates every man's mind and somewhere along the line he will follow this ray back to its central flame. It is this flame that consumes the darkness. Weeping may last for a night but joy comes with the dawn. When darkness disappears the night is as though it never had been. It is everyone's experience Jesus is referring to—yours, mine, all of us.

He tells us that that which is good brings forth goodness, that which is corrupt produces evil; that every tree that brings not forth good fruit is hewn down; that it is he who does the will of God rather than he who says, "Lord, Lord," who enters in. The teaching of Jesus winnows the soul bare. It lays the mind open. It is as relentless as truth. Yet it is permeated with the breath of heaven.

The Kingdom of God which he believed in, lived in, and talked about, is a kingdom that exists today, a kingdom that may be entered into now. We are as immortal now as we ever can become. Time is some part of eternity. It is the entering into conscious union with eternity that gives significance to time. When we find the right relationship with time we shall also be finding a right relationship with eternity.

It is a self-evident proposition that we cannot contract the Infinite but we may expand the finite. We cannot make God in the image of man but we can find man in the image of God. Jesus believed in a power and a presence that all may enter into, but this power can be delivered only on the terms of the nature of the presence. This presence is love, this power is law.

"The kingdom of God cometh not with observation, neither shall they say, Lo here, nor Lo there, for behold! the kingdom of God is within you." This Kingdom is already established. We are in it and its divine nature is incarnated in us. It is neither Lo here, nor Lo there, as though the Kingdom were external, but rather, to the contented heart comes that peace which passeth understanding. "The universe remains to the heart unhurt."

If we had to search for God, where would we go? If we had to find the Kingdom, in what direction should we look? The Illumined One said the Kingdom is within. This Kingdom is already established even though we have not discovered it. Life has made a gift which we have not accepted.

There is an interior reality to everything. A divine pattern is hidden in everything. There is a unifying Presence and Law at the center of everyone and everything, a unity which binds all together in one common source, one living Spirit, one Divine Presence. Each is a unique manifestation of this One. The One wears many faces but behind the mask of each is the co-ordinating unity of all.

Jesus implies that no one can enter the Kingdom of God without desiring to take all others with him, for he said, "I was ahungered, and ye gave me meat; I was thirsty, and ye gave me drink; I was a stranger, and ye took me in; naked, and ye clothed me. I was sick, and ye visited me; I was in prison, and ye came unto me." The Kingdom of God into which he invites us to enter is that realm of pure Spirit which includes everyone. It is a unity of good. It is one of the supreme tests of the integrity of our spiritual conviction that we desire and permit this inclusiveness.

The disciples asked him when was he hungered, when did they feed him and give him to drink, when was he in prison or naked? He answered, "Inasmuch as ye have done it unto one of the least of these . . . ye have done it unto me." As there is one universal Fatherhood so there is one universal Sonship. Each one is an individual member of this Sonship. None is excluded. The least is equal to the greatest and the last is as the first. Therefore, Jesus said that when we do it unto the least we are also doing it unto the greatest.

The Master adds in this same discourse that those who would not take in the stranger or feed the hungry or give the thirsty to drink are cast into outer darkness. Many have interpreted this as a description of a last judgment when the righteous are brought into the household of God and the unrighteous are cast into everlasting punishment. However, this is not the case. "Outer darkness" means standing in the shade, withdrawn from the light. "Punishment" means a process of purification. "Everlasting" means to the end of the age of unrighteousness.

It is useless for us to bemoan the past. We should not condemn ourselves because we have not sooner found the way. Letting the dead bury the dead, with calm, buoyant and abiding faith and trust, with a joyous and enthusiastic expectancy, we should begin to live as though Jesus really knew what he was talking about. Letting all our yesterdays flow backward into the oblivion of previous experience, we should enter the river of life, knowing that it flows free, pure and full from the perennial fountain of our being.

The altar at which the Great Teacher tells us to worship is an altar of faith, hope and trust in the eternal goodness from which alone can come peace. But he said, "If any man will come after me, let him deny himself, and take up his cross, and follow me."

How shall we reconcile the idea of taking up one's cross to follow Jesus with that other exclamation, "My yoke is easy, and my burden is light"? Only by realizing that the cross was a symbol of the Tree of Life, the unity of God with man. The man that must be denied is the one who fails to realize this unity. ". . . whosoever shall save his life shall lose it, and whosoever will lose his life for my sake shall find it . . . for every man is rewarded according to his works."

The song of hate must be laid down if we are to sing a hymn of praise. We must let go of any sense of separation from good if we are to become conscious of union with God. Unity and disunity do not meet at any point. The great hope Jesus lays before us is that we may enter into the Kingdom here and now. The refusal to enter is ours, not God's. If we pass from this life under the judgment of that refusal, we shall have gained nothing. Somewhere, sometime, somehow, the great surrender to life must be made.

We have thought of this surrender in a morbid way, as though joy must go out of our lives and pleasure be subordinated to severity. This could not have been the concept of the one who said, "Peace I leave with you . . . my joy I give unto you." Again and again Jesus tells us that the key that unlocks the golden door to the land of hope is already held in the hand of spiritual awareness.

Our ascent from a material to a spiritual perception of life may not be an easy one but we must make it. We are like a balloon tied to the earth. It impatiently sways in the wind. Something within is pushing it upward, yet it is weighted down. Remove the weights and it bounds upward without effort.

Care and fear weigh us down. Doubt and uncertainty bind us until even hope becomes despair and faith is so burdened with fear that it cannot lift itself into realization. We must learn to loose these burdens, to let go of these weights, to untie the knots that bind us. There is a divine buoyancy within which is lighter than all our burdens, but it cannot carry these burdens upward. It is when we loose them that we are lifted up into the natural atmosphere of our true being.

Perhaps few passages have been so misinterpreted as the one where the Master said that what is bound on earth shall be bound in heaven and what is loosed on earth shall be loosed in heaven. So many have labored under the delusion that Jesus was talking about a literal heaven and hell, vulgarized by theology and used to torment the innocent and confuse the ignorant.

Such a concept will not coincide with the consciousness of one who said to a thief upon another cross, "To day shalt thou be with me in paradise," but rather, should be construed to mean that physical death does not necessarily change our consciousness. Somewhere we must awake to the truth of our being and consciously unify ourselves with things as they really are.

Jesus was a man of strong emotions as well as firm convictions. Because he had been rejected by his own people he wept over Jerusalem, saying, " . . .

how often would I have gathered thy children together, even as a hen gathereth her chickens under her wings, and ye would not." This burst of feeling, coming from one with such tremendous strength of character, shows how human Jesus was. And he adds this stern and pathetic rebuke: "And ye would not." Therefore, "your house is left unto you desolate."

This accusation, "Ye would not," is laid against the doorway of everyone's life, for we all refuse the divine protection and guidance after which we so earnestly seek. We are so confused and blinded by our sense of isolation that it is difficult for us to be gathered under the protective wings of love. Our house is left desolate unto us because it is not roofed with faith. The lamp of hope is not kept burning. The wick of our individual being is withdrawn from the universal oil. Our house is left unto us desolate because its foundation is not laid in a conscious perception of the unity of God with man. Our house is left unto us desolate because its windows are not clean that the mind may become the window of the soul. The door of our upper chamber is locked and inspiration cannot enter.

"There shall not be left here one stone upon another that shall not be thrown down." It was the false construction that Jesus was referring to when he said that not one stone should be left on another.

Everything that is not built on faith, unity, love and law must be "thrown down." He would not have us destroy that which is real. He would have us rebuild our lives on the foundation of the Fatherhood of God and the brotherhood of man.

Time will come again and again, and time will run out again and again, until this spiritual foundation is laid. There is something inexorable about the law of cause and effect which will see to it that not one stone is left unturned until our temple is erected in a likeness of the Divine Pattern.

As individuals we cannot wait for the whole mass of humanity properly to interpret the blueprint of the Divine Plan. When enough individuals have built rightly the vast throng, waiting for something that can restore their faith, will likewise begin to build. It is the duty, the obligation and the privilege of each to rebuild his own temple, casting aside all counterfeit material and supplying it with that true material which is formed from the substance of love, of co-operation and of peace.

Everyone possesses an integrity within himself which no one but himself can violate. Everyone holds a key to the Kingdom in his own hand. No one can live by proxy. Everyone stands naked and alone. Everyone has life within himself. This is why the Great Wayshower tells us to have "salt" in ourselves, to look up to the Spirit that overshadows and within to the Spirit that indwells.

The communion of the soul with its Source comes through the recognition that the innermost spirit of man is an incarnation of God—Christ manifesting himself in humanity. It is this inward life that is the "salt" within us. That which gives savor to life, that divine ingredient which must be diffused in all our acts.

It is a direct relationship of the individual to the Universal, of the earthly son to his heavenly Father, that Jesus accentuated. In one of his most subtle instructions he said that if we confess our relationship to him (to Christ) he will confess this same relationship before God, but if we deny it he also will deny it. When we seek the high altitude of spiritual realization we find that Christ (the spirit of Truth within us) becomes an automatic mediator between our personal lives and the creative Spirit Itself.

When we deny this unity before men, that is, when our thoughts and acts arise from doubt and unbelief, then our denial of the Divine Presence inhibits Its action through our lives. Thus our lack of confession through outward act and inward thought denies us before our Father which is in heaven—not eternally, of course, but temporarily.

There is nothing between us and the Kingdom of

God but our own mistakes. We cancel these mistakes through no longer indulging in them. Through Christ we receive inspiration and hope, and, no matter what the obstructions encountered, the power to overcome them through faith and childlike trust. It is certain that we cannot carry our mistakes into the Kingdom of Good nor can we cause that Kingdom to enter into our mistakes. Heaven is not reached in this manner.

Jesus said who loses his life shall find it. Of course, he was not referring to the real life which cannot be lost, for it is forever hid with Christ in God. Let us apply this thought to one of the most commonplace of all our experiences—the consciousness of fear, uncertainty and insecurity which is at the base of so much trouble. If we have been living in fear we must cease feeding this fear upon the life force that is within us. We must lose it if we would find peace.

Somewhere along the line of our evolution we must surrender our doubts. Somewhere in the journey of life we shall be called upon to separate ourselves from the body of our false beliefs. Is this not what the Apostle meant when he said, "I die daily"? Not that life dies. It is that part of us which we have given a temporary life to, in the form of negation, that must cease to exist. The Apostle speaks of this as a war between the spirit and the flesh.

Jesus refers to it in a more lenient manner because

he was a man of peace. His followers were filled
with enthusiasm and zeal and with an almost fanati-
cal impulsion. There was nothing wrong about this.
It was their way of putting off the old man. But the
Master, being a man of tranquillity, taught us a better method, so simple that it almost eludes us. In
essence he said: "Think about God and God will
think about you. Turn from your mistakes, turn in
thought to God, and God will turn to you."

When we turn from destructive emotions they
are no longer fed by the creative imagination. A
transformation takes place when love destroys hate
by absorbing it in its divine flame. The negative
state which we have created by unhappiness cannot
be healed by adding more unhappiness nor by an-
alyzing the unhappiness we already have. Rather, it
is healed as we turn to the contemplation of wholeness. Filling the consciousness with joy lifts grief out
of itself until it no longer exists.

Jesus said that whatever offends must be cast off,
be it a hand, a foot or an eye. The false seeing must
be done away with, as well as the wrong doing.
Where the eye offends it must be plucked out, and
where the hand offends it must be cut off and cast
forth. This is a word picture telling us that when
we seek the Kingdom we must resolutely cast aside
everything that inhibits the divine light. The Wayshower referred to this childlike consciousness when

he said, "In heaven their angels do always behold the face of my Father which is in heaven."

Suppose we think of "their angels" as our own spiritual being. Socrates spoke of a spirit which accompanied him. The Greek philosophers spoke of the spiritual prototype of one's life as being "over yonder," meaning in heaven. Jesus referred to the angel of the real self, to that part of us that does behold the face of God, that part of us that has never left its heaven. This is what Wordsworth meant when he said that we come from heaven, "not in complete nakedness or forgetfulness but trailing clouds of glory." There is something in us that always remembers "that celestial palace whence we came."

To believe that through faith that which seems so far from its heavenly home can behold its Father's face forevermore, is not only one of the greatest concepts we can entertain, it is one of the most glorified. Jesus told us also that we are born from the Kingdom of God, that it is around, about and within us, that there is some part of our being which eternally exists in the bosom of the Father, in a state of harmony.

There is a guardian angel that accompanies everyone through life. It is the angel of God's presence in that person. It is his spiritual nature. If we believe that the Divine Spirit is incarnated in us—and how could we exist unless It were?—then, with Jesus, we would have to accept that there is some part of us which does behold the face of God forevermore.

Our spiritual hand already is placed in the hand of the heavenly Father. It is our human hands that are weak. These are the hands that the Wise One tells us must be cast off. It is our human vision that sees confusion. It is these eyes he tells us must be plucked out. The human hand must be placed in the hand of God and the physical vision transmuted into a divine seeing which beholds the Kingdom of God, not only in our infancy, but in our maturity. We must catch this vision which can guide us not only to the western circle where our earthly sun sets, but beyond this horizon to an eternal dawn.

No life is worth living without this faith. No intellect, however great, can fulfill its proper office without this inspiration. No consciousness, no matter what else it may have gathered in this world, can function with spiritual sanity unless it believes in this guidance.

There is a place in the soul where the ocean of life comes to a crest and individualizes itself in us. Below the crest of this wave is the whole ocean. Intuitively we seek to reunite with it, not to a loss of the self but to the finding of the self immersed in, and one with, the Universal Being. There is an urge behind all our acts pressing us back to this center. There is an intuition echoing through all our thoughts telling us that there is such a center. There is a testimony in the soul proclaiming the integrity of our conviction.

We are all familiar with the story of Nicodemus who came at night to the Master for spiritual guidance. He must have asked about the Kingdom of Heaven for Jesus answered, "Except a man be born again he cannot see the kingdom of God." And Nicodemus asked, "How can a man be born when he is old?" The answer was: "Except a man be born of water and of spirit, he cannot enter into the kingdom of God."

In the ancient spiritual philosophy of the Jews it was said that there are three Adams—the Adam of the earth, the Adam of the air, and the Adam of the sky. "The first Adam is of this earth, the last Adam is the Lord from heaven." All of this seems very mysterious until we understand its meaning. We have a spiritual nature, a psychical nature, and a physical nature. One side of our being is hid with Christ in God. The other side seems to walk solidly upon the earth. Between these two stretches the mind, which touches both sides.

It is the mind to which Jesus refers when he says that we must be born of water as well as of spirit. The mind is the creative process within us. When it thinks only from the standpoint of externals it automatically encloses us in a prison of limitation.

When it receives inspiration from on High, and through intuition thinks the thoughts of God after Him, it imparts new vigor to body and circumstance.

Jesus knew more about these things than any other person who ever lived and when he said, "You must be born of water and of spirit," he meant that the mind must be converted through an influx of the Spirit. Nicodemus was a teacher and ruler but apparently he did not understand the ancient instruction of his own temple, that man is a threefold being of spirit, soul or mind, and body. As a teacher he should have understood what Jesus was talking about. He should have known that the physical universe is an outpicturing of ideas held in the Divine Mind. He should have understood that everything in nature has a corresponding cause in the invisible.

The Master was trying to show him that just as we are born physically through natural laws, so may we be reborn mentally through spiritual law. He said that which is born of the flesh is flesh, and that which is born of the spirit is spirit, and he plainly told Nicodemus how to be born of the spirit when he said, "The wind bloweth where it listeth, and thou hearest the sound thereof, but canst not tell whence it cometh or whither it goeth; so is everyone that is born of the spirit."

And now comes one of the most remarkable utterances of this illumined soul: "And no man hath ascended up to heaven, but he that came down from heaven, even the Son of man which is in heaven." Stated in non-mystical language this is equal to saying that no man could go to heaven unless he had come from heaven; he could neither go to heaven nor have come from heaven unless he were already in heaven.

This we recognize as a reiteration of the teaching of the threefold nature of man—the Adam of the earth, the air and the sky, or, spirit, soul and body. There is some part of us that has never completely descended from heaven—this is our spirit; some part of us that is suspended between heaven and earth—this is the mind; and the physical that stands upon the earth—this is the body.

The body could not receive direction from the mind unless it were in immediate, corresponding and parallel connection with it, nor could the mind receive inspiration from the Spirit unless it were in immediate connection with It. Therefore, most of the ancient systems taught that the mind is the medium or mediator between the spiritual and the physical.

The remarkable thing about the teaching of Jesus was that he viewed this threefold nature of our being as an everpresent reality. We are spirits now as much as we shall ever become. We have a mind now and do not need to acquire one. We have a body and this body is not an illusion. The universe is a spiritual system and a unitary wholeness. The Spirit expresses Itself in terms of intelligence, while intelligence acts as law, projecting form.

Jesus tells us that man is of like nature to the Supreme Spirit Itself. He tells us that when the son of man is lifted up he will cease to perish and enter into eternal life. He did not say that when he is lifted up he will become immortal, but rather, through being lifted up he enters into an immortality which already exists. We cannot become something that we are not.

We may only increasingly become aware of what we are, and Jesus plainly shows that this becoming aware is a lifting up of the consciousness to that which already is. All human progress is a result of becoming increasingly aware of powers and potentialities that eternally exist in a changeless universe. The Spirit Itself is not evolving, but man is becoming increasingly aware of those laws that had no beginning and can have no end.

Everything that the Great Revelator taught will have a deeper meaning if we keep in mind that the spiritual universe was as real to him as the physical universe is to us. If we lift up our consciousness to the Divine we are lifting up the son within us to a perception of his union with God. When we believe in this son as begotten of the love of God we cease to perish and enter into a consciousness of eternal existence here and now.

Jesus said that God did not send His son to condemn the world but to save it. The great condemnation is that we fail to see the light because our deeds are evil. But he added, " . . . he that doeth truth cometh to the light that his deeds may be made manifest, that they are wrought in God." Here again we find his teaching of parallels. Coming into the light which God is, entering into close and conscious communion with the love which God must be, we enter into a newness of life, permitting the divine energy to flow through our will and imagination into act, thus causing our act to be "wrought in God."

No other man ever issued so great an invitation, and none was so able to prove the claim he made upon God—the immediate availability of good, but the power of good acting as immutable law in human experience.

The Great Savior, the True Redeemer, the Master Mind of the ages, a living embodiment of God in man, comes with a dramatic appeal, with divine authority, with a consciousness of love and a word of power, and proclaims that there is a way, a truth and a life; that there is a celestial fire forever emanating from the center of things. He says, in effect: "Follow your light back and you will find the flame.

Follow your individual stream and you will find its perennial source springing spontaneously within you." He says plainly that we may regain our lost paradise, and do so here and now.

Naturally, we are enthusiastic, we are filled with hope, and we set about the return journey with gladness. However, we soon find that those things which contradict the Divine Nature must be dropped, that we can no longer be burdened with fear, doubt or uncertainty; that we can no longer be burdened with anything that can hurt, for the Kingdom of God is as harmless as an innocent child. Therefore, he tells us that we must be born again.

There is travail in this new birth, not to the Spirit but to the emotions and the intellect. There is a terrific wrench when we separate ourselves from that which must be left behind if we would be born again. We find that love knows nothing about hate. We must leave hate behind. We must wrench it from our psyche, tear it loose from its moorings in our mental and emotional lives.

We discover that confusion cannot enter peace, that fear has no affinity with faith. One by one the great negations of life must be loosed from the soul. It must come pure and clean and fresh. It must come in calm confidence and in complete trust. It must come with anticipation, hope and acceptance. And it must come now and not by and by.

This is the great teaching of Jesus: the fields are white unto the harvest now. Tomorrow will be another *now* when it becomes today. Tomorrow is but *now* stretched into the future, even as today is but the lengthened shadow of yesterday. There is a now which is eternal. There is a today, and only a today, in which we may enter into the heavenly Kingdom. We need not worry about tomorrow—"sufficient unto the day is the evil thereof." We need not worry about yesterday—"your sins are forgiven you." But we must be right today. We are to separate ourselves from the mistakes of yesterday and avoid the fears of tomorrow. Today life starts fresh and new. We are born anew each day. Every day is a fresh beginning.

Thus today springs up into everlasting life, here and now. "Verily I say unto you, he that heareth my word, and believeth on him that sent me, hath everlasting life, and shall not come into condemnation, but is passed from death into life." Let us note that the Master did not say, "He *shall* pass through death into life." He plainly states, "He *has* passed *from* death *into* life."

The whole instruction of Jesus was to the effect that the Kingdom is present with us now in all its fullness. The truth he talked about not only includes immortality and the going on of the individual soul, it also includes a provision for our needs at every step of the journey, here or hereafter. The Kingdom is at hand, and the substance of that Kingdom is flowing. The love of God is not a far-off event but a present reality. The divine outpouring is eternally taking place. The Illumined One conceived the table of life to be spread with the gifts of heaven and invites all to sup with him, not by and by, but this very moment. Could it be possible that we are already at the banquet table of heaven and refusing to eat?

This seems too good to be true, but everything that this glorified soul told us seems too good to be true. Have we acted as though Jesus really knew what he was talking about? Have we tried to follow those footsteps which left an imprint on the sands of time that nothing can obliterate?

CHAPTER VII

The Prayer of Faith

AT THE time when Jesus lived it was the custom to stand at the street corners and pray, using a loud voice, petitioning God with vehemence, sometimes in fear but always with reverence. This rather noisy approach to the Spirit did not disturb the Master. Knowing that everyone is rewarded according to his faith, he said, "Verily I say unto you, They have their reward."

What magnificent understanding! What depth of reason! What profound insight into the nature of reality! The one who knew God did not condemn any man's way of approaching the Source of all being, but in teaching his more intimate followers, those to whom he said it was given "to know the mysteries of the kingdom," he counselled a calm, simple, direct and childlike trust in God.

First of all, he said, "Judge not according to appearances." That is, do not be confused by the conditions around you. Prayer always reaches its highest possibility when it rises above the limitation of any existing circumstance. Jesus had this kind of faith. How could anyone arrive at such a conviction unless he knew that he was dealing with a Power which can re-arrange facts and create new ones?

A belief in the power of the Invisible is the very essence of faith. Prayer, or spiritual communion, demands a complete surrender. Because the creative power of God is at hand, all things are possible. Man is powerful because he deals with Power. He may become wise because he is immersed in Wisdom. Thus he has an inexhaustible Source from which to draw both power and wisdom. The purpose of prayer, or spiritual communion, is to seek conscious union with the indwelling Presence.

Sometimes we arrive merely at a partial unity with Spirit. At other times this union is more complete. Always our prayer will be as effective as is the realization generated through the act of communion. When the realization is complete our words become "clothed upon" with the living Presence of an invisible Power ever projecting Itself into form through our meditation.

Spiritual communion is deeper than intellectual perception. The prayer of the intellect may be perfect in form, but it must be warmed and colored by feeling and conviction. We must cast off all intellectual doubts if we would enter into a deep, spiritual communion with Reality.

In no way should this be considered a censure of the intellect, for we are given intelligence as an instrument of choice, decision and action. But it is only when this intelligence has in the background a deep feeling, almost an artistic sense of an immense beauty, that it really reflects the Divine Nature. Jesus was one of those rare persons who, without lessening the integrity of his intellect, made it a mouthpiece for the Spirit. "I thank thee, O Father, lord of heaven and earth, because thou hast hid these things from the wise and prudent, and hast revealed them unto babes."

The simplicity of this childlike trust was one of the outstanding qualities of the Great Teacher. Intellectual knowledge alone, desirable as it is, is not sufficient. We must reach a place where in simple trust we turn to the Spirit as a child to its parent—the instinctive sense which turns to its mother for food or to its father for strength. This is the attitude Jesus would have us assume toward God.

And he spoke about a Pharisee and a publican who went up to the temple to pray. The Pharisee prayed aloud, saying, "God, I thank thee that I am not as other men," while the publican smote upon his breast, saying, "God, be merciful to me, a sinner." The Master told his followers that the publican and not the Pharisee was justified in his attitude toward God, "for everyone that exalteth himself shall be abased, and he that humbleth himself shall be exalted." Jesus did not condemn the Pharisee. He did praise the publican. The prayer of one was spoken to be heard of men; the prayer of the other was a confession of weakness seeking divine strength.

There should be a true humility in our approach to life and to God—a humility based on the grandeur of things; the humility of a man of science approaching a principle of nature or a mathematician trying to measure the unimaginable reaches of space. It is the humility of a surrender of the lesser to the greater, of a part to the whole.

To sin means to make a mistake. We all make mistakes, therefore we all sin. To deny that we make mistakes is but a psychological attempt to cover up our unconscious sense of guilt because of the mistakes we have made. To gain relief from this sense of guilt we may scream our prayers into the infinite, we may boldly assert that we are not as other men. This self-righteousness, however, is but a psychological aggression built up as a defense mechanism against an inward sense of guilt. The publican who came down from the temple, having humbly proclaimed himself a sinner, had found a release from psychic tensions and burdens which the arrogance of the Pharisee never could have found.

True spiritual humility is not humbling oneself before a despotic power which seeks to avenge itself against our shortcomings. It is a submission of the lesser to the greater, of the finite to the infinite. This submission makes possible a more complete, conscious union with God. Throughout the ages and in many modern spiritual institutions confession is a common practice, and a salutary one. But possibly there is a deeper catharsis of the psyche than this—a searching of the soul which no one can do for us but ourselves; an inward sense of being right with the universe.

Jesus said that our relationship to God should be personal and direct. We regain our lost paradise of childlike faith and walk the golden shores of peace only when we feel ourselves close to the ocean of love. Since Divine Wisdom has seen fit to make us individuals, it is only as each follows the individual current of his consciousness back to its source and discovers a union forever made that he can find complete release from a sense of condemnation. The publican found such a release when he smote his chest and said, "God, be merciful to me, a sinner."

In words so simple that the vast mass of persons heard him gladly, Jesus taught that God is Infinite Spirit, personal to us and responding to us. It was the very simplicity of his thought that appealed to people. Yet, when we analyze his teaching, we find a profoundness, a depth of feeling, a logic and a mathematics that could well engage the attention of the deepest intellects of the ages. As a matter of fact, we have not at all fathomed its depth. Its very simplicity has eluded us.

Nature has given us confidence. We acquire fear. What strain and anguish we would avoid if we could maintain a simple attitude of trust. We have this childlike trust in the laws of nature. We expect the law of gravitation to hold us in place. We expect our parents to care for us and our friends to love us. Jesus tells us to have an equal faith in God.

We should practice this childlike faith. The results will be worth many times the effort. With confidence, with a simplicity of approach and a glad and spontaneous recognition, let us recapture the sense of security of our childhood days. The more burdened the mind, the more necessary it is to find a place in consciousness which is free from fear, doubt and uncertainty.

It was this faith which Jesus spoke of when he said that just as we have earthly fathers who care for us, so we may be certain that our Father in heaven has an equal and a deeper love for us. "Suffer the little children to come unto me, and forbid them not, for of such is the kingdom of heaven." Would that we might enter this Kingdom, that we might recapture this, the greatest good of all—a simple faith in life.

We all feel the need of an intimate and personal relationship with the Spirit. We need the personal experience, not only of conscious communion with God, but equally we need the assurance that God will respond. We must feel that when we talk to the Spirit we actually commune with It; otherwise, we shall have no sense of personal response. Communion means that something goes out and something returns; that we not only seek Him but that we find Him. There is no such thing as a one-sided communion. Unless the response is there, the attempt to hold communion ends in emptiness and futility. We must gain the assurance that God not only hears, He answers; that we are not talking to a vacuum or attempting to commune with the emptiness of space.

Jesus said that all space is filled with the Divine Presence peopling Itself with the many forms of Its own creation. He taught that all things and all people are rooted in this Divine Intelligence, which, because It is individualized in each, is personal to all.

Coupled with this concept of the Divine Presence and our relationship to It, he taught a universal law of cause and effect, a law of mind in action, operating creatively upon our thought. "Thy faith hath made thee whole . . . Believe and it shall be done." These statements refer to an impersonal law operating on our belief. This mental and spiritual principle in nature responds to us by *corresponding* with our mental attitudes toward life. This is the law that causes faith to become fact in our experience.

"It is done unto you as you believe" not only implies something which responds, its response is actually limited to our belief. It not only responds *to* us, but it responds to us *as* we believe. It responds by co-respondence, by reflection, as placing an image in front of a mirror causes it to reflect the image. The reflection is identical with the image. The reflection is as the image compels it to be. The image is a cause, the reflection an effect. The image does not make itself. We can shift the image in front of a mirror and the reflection automatically will change to correspond with the new image.

So Jesus referred to the prayer of faith as that which causes a creative law to reflect back to us the situations and conditions corresponding with our beliefs. There is no way to interpret the statement, "It is done unto you as you believe," other than to accept it in its utmost simplicity and take it for granted that it means what the words imply.

The conclusion is inevitable. There is a mental and spiritual law which operates upon our thought. This concept was explicit in the consciousness of Jesus when he said, "It is done unto you as you believe," and in many other statements where he spoke of the action of faith.

Later Paul devoted a whole section of his instruction to the need of faith, telling of the mighty works that had been accomplished through belief. And he added that when any man asks of God who "giveth to all men liberally . . . let him ask in faith, nothing wavering, for he that wavereth is like a wave of the sea driven by the wind and tossed. Let not that man think that he shall receive anything of the Lord" for "a double minded man is unstable in all his ways."

"Faith is the substance of things hoped for, the evidence of things not seen," Paul exclaimed. It would be difficult to find a better explanation of faith. After having shown what faith had done through the ages, he analyzed its meaning and stated that it is both evidence and substance. It is evidence in that it produces a practical result. It is substance in that it can take form in our affairs.

"The just shall live by faith" and "God is the rewarder of them that diligently seek after him." Surely this is something worth considering. It is but natural that we wish the good things of life. God's Kingdom must include everything that is worth while as well as everything that is worthy. Being substance it must include supply, that daily manna necessary to our physical sustenance. Being the essence of life it must include all possible livingness. Being the original architect it must include the spiritual patterns of everything. Being the giver of life it must be the great physician whose benediction of love includes the healing of our physical infirmities.

Jesus emphasized the need of using faith through love; James of using faith through reason. Paul said that faith, being substance, produces its own evidence. From these three we may conclude that faith, through love and reason, can produce any desired personal good, provided that personal desire does not contradict the nature of reality itself. Faith through love and reason, then, is a key that unlocks the divine storehouse. We cannot doubt that this storehouse is filled with every heavenly blessing, including our daily food, clothing and shelter, the healing of our bodies, harmony in our affairs as well as unity and love in our human relationships.

We should study to have faith, not as an abstract quality of the mind, but as an active agency in the thought, in everything we do, say and think. In the lives of those who have had faith we find examples worthy to follow. But we dare not stop here. The lives of others should remind us of the latent possibility within ourselves. Great examples are but signposts on the pathway of our own spiritual evolution. We should study, therefore, to have faith for ourselves. We should practice faith.

Reducing it to its utmost simplicity, faith resolves itself into a mental attitude toward life. It is a certain, positive and affirmative way of thinking. But too often faith is contaminated by unbelief which flows out of the collective experience of the human race. We say that certain things cannot be because they never have been. It is self-evident that such conclusions are wrong for our present knowledge of physical, mental and spiritual laws contradicts the common experience of the ages preceding us.

Jesus and his immediate followers boldly asserted that a mental attitude of faith, arrived at through love, can perform miracles. These miracles are in accord with the immutable law of cause and effect that governs everything. Law governs faith just as law governs everything else in the universe.

Spiritual faith is unshakable conviction, a surrender of the mind, the will and the imagination to the belief in an invisible agency which can and will respond to us. To study to have faith should be one of our main endeavors. The rules for the use of faith are definitely laid down in the teaching of Jesus and his immediate followers. We must either set the whole story aside as a myth, dissipate its meaning through thinking of it as impossible of attainment, or accept it as a simple, understandable, concise method of procedure.

The placing of faith in the category of the impossible annihilates such hope as we might have. The placing of it in the realm of the possible, fires the mind with determination, buoys the hope with expectancy, and gives creative impulse to the imagination.

If one is to have faith he must first have it within himself. He must deliberately decide that he is going to live by faith, and he must consciously train himself into a new way of thinking. As surely as he does this, definite results will take place in his experience. There will be an evidence which gives substance to his belief.

We should start on this, perhaps the greatest of all adventures, with a firm conviction in its reality and with a will to follow it through. This would be praying without ceasing. But this does not mean that we retire from living. It means that even in the most commonplace experience we add a little more faith to our present hope and expectancy. Daily we should grow into a greater assurance, a more complete reliance upon the Spirit. As our conviction grows our experiences are brought more and more under control of the law of good. Gradually we come to know what the hope of the ages has longed for.

One day there came to Jesus "a certain man, kneeling down to him, and saying, Have mercy on my son, for he is a lunatic." He had already brought his son to the disciples but they were unable to restore him. Jesus answered the man and said, "O faithless and perverse generation! How long shall I be with you? How long shall I suffer you? Bring him hither to me." He rebuked the evil spirit and it came out and the young man was instantly restored to sanity.

This is one of the few instances where Jesus was impatient. It was not an impatience with his followers but with their ignorance. When they asked him why they could not heal the young man he replied, "Because of your unbelief," for, he said, if their faith were as a grain of mustard seed they could remove mountains. "Howbeit this kind goeth not out but by prayer and fasting."

It is difficult to grasp the full significance of a life completely surrendered to faith. Jesus depended so much on spiritual means and methods. He did this without denying physical laws and without denying the reality of the physical universe.

He never explained away disease, poverty, unhappiness or other human experiences. Instead of explaining them *away,* he *explained* them in light of the concept that the manifest universe is a logical and inevitable result of the contemplation of God and that each person's individual experience is a necessary counterpart of his own consciousness. He explained that as consciousness is lifted to spiritual perception it revitalizes experience and projects harmony in the place of discord.

All things are possible to faith when it permits the spiritual pattern to flow through it into harmonious self-expression. What we have to overcome is not conditions in themselves but the thought that there is any power opposed to good or any presence other than the presence of perfect life. To some this may seem folly. To Jesus it was the great reality.

When he told his disciples that this kind comes out but by fasting and prayer he was explaining that the greater the confusion which confronts us, the more complete must be our surrender to peace. The more dense the obstruction, the more completely must we penetrate it with spiritual vision. Fasting and prayer lift consciousness to greater heights. This does not necessarily mean fasting from food nor prayer to the exclusion of performance. It is a lifting up of consciousness until we behold the face of Truth and not its mask.

In his Epistle to the Romans Paul says, "The just shall live by faith . . . for the invisible things of him (God) from the creation of the world are clearly seen, being understood by the things that are made . . ." This passage is an emphasis of the philosophy of Jesus. The just shall live by faith. The invisible things of God are made manifest in the visible. This means the prototypes or divine patterns. Things in the visible world have their cause in the invisible.

Faith in the invisible permits the spiritual prototype to come to the surface. The prototype itself is not seen with the physical eye. It is invisible from the foundation of the world because we do not see causation. The very fact that it produces an effect is ample proof of its existence.

On one of his journeys a woman who had been diseased for twelve years came behind Jesus and touched the hem of his garment, saying within herself, "If I may but touch his garment, I shall be whole." How simple was her faith, surrendering doubt and fear to the inspiration she received from one who was pure in heart, perfect in vision and divine in forgiveness. Jesus, knowing that her need had stretched forth a hand of acceptance, told her that her faith had restored her.

Why did not the Master say, "*My* faith has restored you"? It was because he knew that all people are alike in the sight of God that he told the woman her own faith had healed her. Would that this thought might come to the millions whose hands are reaching out to touch the seamless robe of Truth! The simple act of faith becomes a channel for the Divine Life to flow through us. The just and the pure in heart live by faith.

The vision of Jesus we should catch is not merely one of a glorious figure who so calmly and majestically trod the human pathway, but of the lesson he brought: "Behold, I am with you alway, even unto the end of the world." This "I AM" is the presence of God at the center of every person's life. It is this Divine Presence which is with us always. The inspired personality of the Great Teacher has long since departed. The presence in which he consciously lived and with which he communed, and the Divine Law which he so compassionately used, is ours for the taking, today and every day.

But we cannot pour the new wine of spiritual inspiration into old bottles of morbid introspection. We must let the mistakes of yesterday disappear into new seasons, new grapes, new wine, new life for old, hope for despair, faith for fear, love for hate. The healing of our wounds, be they of body or mind, comes through the outpouring of that Spirit whose season of fruitage is perennial, filling our expectation to overflowing and placing upon us the garment of hope for the shroud of despair. If we wish this miracle to take place we must first believe that it can.

The human mind needs, and must have, a direct approach to God, to this invisible Presence we call Life, to this Divine Being we call Spirit. It is natural for us to reach out from our ignorance to Its enlightenment, from our weakness to Its strength, from our darkness to Its light. We should feel and know that the Spirit is right where we are; that if we let It operate through us all will be well.

The disciples of Jesus, watching him in his ministry to the sick and ignorant, among those common people who heard him so gladly, asked him to teach them how to pray. They had seen new light come into the eyes of those whose vision was dim. They had seen new energy flowing through the limbs of the paralyzed. They had seen the lame walk, the dumb speak and the deaf hear. And so they asked how to pray with power.

The Master knew, as we all know, that no one can go outside himself. If he goes up in the mountain, he will still be himself. If he goes into the temple and throws himself in front of the altar, he will still be himself. Every man will have to find God in his own way. It would be a rash and foolish person who would assume that his is the sole and only right way. It may be right for him, of course, and he should follow it. Through doing this he will come to know God. All ways that lead to God are right.

Jesus answered their inquiry by telling them that when they prayed they should, having shut out all appearances to the contrary, enter the closet. He was not referring to a physical room or hiding place. To enter the closet means to withdraw into one's own thought, to shut out all confusion and discord. Here in the silence of the soul one looks to the all-creative Wisdom and Power. When we have entered this closet and shut the door to outward appearances we are to make known our requests—"what things soever ye desire."

Next we are told that we should *believe that we actually possess* the object of our desire, disregarding all appearances to the contrary. When we enter into our invisible inheritance, acting as though it were true, our faith will take on actual form. The Divine Giver Himself will make the gift, but first we must believe. ". . . believe that ye receive them, and ye shall have them."

This is a veiled statement of the law of cause and effect operating in human affairs. Having made known our request with thanksgiving and received the answer with gratitude, we should rest assured that the law of good will bring about the desired result.

The Great Wayshower said that the way to approach God is direct, simple, and now. The amazing thing is that every man is exactly where Jesus said he must go. He is there already. He does not have to go anywhere; he begins where he is. Jesus said we should go inside ourselves. He called this "entering the closet"—closing our eyes to all externals and thinking and feeling something within.

He said that when we have done this we are then to tell God just what we want. And when we have told God what we want we are to believe that He is going to give it to us. He was definite about this, for he said that when we ask God for something we should believe not only that He *is* going to give it to us, but that He already *has* given it to us.

Prayer is a movement of consciousness on the uni-

verse itself. It is the law of mind in action. Whenever our acceptance makes it possible there will be an
answer to our prayer which mathematically corresponds to the use we have been making of this law of
mind. Jesus tells us that when we comply with the
law it will be done unto us as we believe. He was
teaching the law of mind in action, the exercise of
the God Power within us as a mathematical sequence
of cause and effect.

But prayer does not concentrate the law, it merely
focalizes our attention on it. We do not gather the
principle of mathematics together or concentrate it
for our use. We merely draw upon it. So it is in the
act of prayer. It is attention and not concentration;
willingness and not will.

If we wish to demonstrate that prayer or spiritual
communion is a potent force, we must believe that
both energy and divine action are at our disposal;
that the creative Genius of the universe is already
wherever we focus our attention. We must *permit*
rather than petition. Spiritual communion is letting
go of negation, a reaching out and up toward freedom, wholeness and happiness. There is no struggle,
no tension—only peace. Since we are dealing with a
Power which can easily accomplish our desired good
and give to us more abundantly even than we are
able to receive, there should be no sense of compul-
sion, but rather, a relaxed yet attentive and active

acceptance. All anxiety should be dropped by the wayside.

Joy infuses the commonplace with creative activity. Jesus spoke of the joy which he had and which he desired his disciples to have, that their joy might be full. There is a song at the center of everything. The music of the spheres is no illusion. We must uncover this song and permit it to saturate our souls with joy. We must let it sing to us.

Enthusiasm is the most creative of all the imaginative faculties. There is something light, unobstructed, weightless about it. We cannot associate the Spirit with sadness or depression. The very thought of the "Fountain of Life" suggests a gushing forth, a bubbling up from a subterranean passage, whose flow is irresistible. Spiritual communion is not a droll affair. It is not a wailing wall. It is the triumphant procession of the soul into the secret place of the Most High.

The creative energy of Spirit must be boundless. Therefore, we can set no limit to the possibility of what It can do for us. It is able to give us infinitely more than we have expected, understood or accepted. It cannot only make the gift, It can, out of Its own energy and power, out of Its own being, create the way, the method and the means through which the gift is to come to us.

Jesus gave the most simple prayer ever uttered, and the only one common to all Christian faiths.

After this manner, therefore, pray ye:

Our Father which art in heaven . . . God is the Father of everyone—not just your Father, or my Father, but *our* Father. Being *our* Father, He is always ready to respond to us. We have a direct relationship to God, right now, while we are on this earth. Jesus said we should come to this heavenly Father just as we would to an earthly one, tell Him what we need, and expect Him to provide a way through which our need may be met.

He had already told his disciples that heaven is within. Our Father is in our heaven and our heaven is already within as well as around us. We can talk to this God who is within us and He will answer. We can ask and we shall receive. We have no power of ourselves, alone, just as an electric generator has no power of itself but is merely an instrument which uses a power caught from nature. Of ourselves we can do nothing, but the Father can do anything.

God must be perfect, happy and whole. God must already have provided everything we need. Our trouble is that we have not learned how to accept. We have not had faith because we have not realized how close God is. We have felt that God has withheld things from us, not realizing that our thought of rejection has made it appear as though He were distant.

And now, according to this marvelous prayer, we are to turn within and find the Divine Presence which is greater than we are, greater than all people combined could possibly be—the one, supreme, absolute and perfect Power. *Our Father which art* means the Power that is, and *Our Father which art in heaven* means that this Power is within us and accessible to us.

Hallowed be thy name. In the exultation of his "jubilant and beholding soul" Jesus proclaimed the wondrous name of God, the ineffable sweetness of the Divine Nature and the glory of Its eternal reign. *Hallowed be thy name* is more than a salutation, it is a song of praise.

Thy kingdom come. God's Kingdom is the kingdom of wholeness. This Kingdom is within us, within everyone; it is everywhere. If the Kingdom is within it must be a Kingdom of the mind. We can accept or reject this Kingdom, but the Kingdom will never reject us. This is why Jesus told us to believe in this Kingdom. Our Kingdom is a kingdom of faith, a kingdom of acceptance and co-operation, a kingdom of love and joy, a kingdom of happiness and success.

We have felt that both God and man have rejected

us. We have become so morbid over this that we have rejected ourselves and condemned ourselves and falsely judged ourselves. Of course, we have done this in ignorance of our true nature.

Now, as our night of ignorance passes into the dawn of understanding, as our sense of being separate from God passes into the realization of the Presence within and around us, should we not lift up our eyes to this heaven in which we believe, and, turning from fear, enter it with faith? Should we not enter with joy and happiness, with a sense of security and peace, with confidence and trust? Just as a child places his hand in the hand of his parent or friend, should we not reach our hands out to God with complete confidence? All who have done this have come to know that there is a presence, a power, a love and a protection upon which they may rely.

Thy will be done . . . Being creations of God, His will for us cannot be other than to express Himself through us. If God is perfect—and who can doubt this—then God could not desire anything for us other than perfection. The will of God for us must be joy and peace, happiness and abundance, health and love, and every other good thing we have dreamed of. If we are the children of God and are like Him in nature, then we may know that He cannot desire us to be unhappy, sick, afraid or impoverished.

. . . *in earth, as it is in heaven.* This is one of the
greatest statements ever made. It could only have
been made by one who had experienced the immediate availability of good, who knew that God is over
all, in all and through all, who had exercised Divine
Power through love and reason; by one who had his
prayers answered. And then for such a man to say
that this is true about everyone because God is the
Father of all, was a fitting climax to the greatest story
ever told—the story of the Divine Partnership we all
have with that Father who has never left us, and who
never will.

The earth belongs to God. Everything in it is controlled by Him. The Kingdom of God on earth is
just as real as the Kingdom of God in heaven, because
heaven is here when we see it. This Kingdom of
Heaven includes our physical bodies, our physical environments, and everything we are doing that is good,
right and just.

Anyone who realises that he already possesses such
a kingdom, and lives in it, must be happy and contented. He will feel safe and secure. He will have a
deep sense of trust. With it will come a peace of
mind, an inward certainty about life, a faith and conviction, and above everything else, a sureness about
his own individual being, his soul. He will come to
know that he is an eternal being now, that he is im-

mortal today. He will begin to live as though he were going to live forever.

When the Kingdom of God is perceived and the Will and Nature of God understood, then shall the Power within us re-create and control our environment after the pattern of wholeness and abundance. When that which is without shall be controlled by that which is within, when the Kingdom of God comes on earth among men, it will heal all nations of sickness, war and poverty, for the Kingdom of God is wholeness, unity and peace.

Give us this day our daily bread. It is God who gives. It is we who receive. Is not this true of all life? Nature gives us seed time and harvest, sunshine and rain, the fruit of the vine. Day by day God gives us everything we need—the gifts of peace, joy and happiness. The divine givingness come from the inexhaustible resources of the Kingdom of Heaven. But since we are self-choosing, we must receive the gift in our own thought. Our fears, lacks, limitations, worries, pathetically suggest how inadequate our receiving has been. To fulfill the Divine Givingness we must set up an equal receivingness.

Our "daily bread" means whatever we need, whenever we need it, wherever we need it, and for as long as we need it. We must not think of our good coming only from employment or investments. These are merely some of the ways God uses to give to us. We have many and varied needs but the source of our supply is One Power. We should not limit God's giving to any particular channel for God can open up channels in our experience every day—new and better ones, "what things soever ye desire."

We must, however, be certain that the desire is consistent with the nature of Reality. We may be certain that if our desire is toward a greater degree of livingness for ourselves and others, and harms no one, then it is aligned with the Divine Will, which means the Divine Nature.

And forgive us our debts, as we forgive our debtors. How can we hope to be forgiven unless we forgive? If we keep on hating we shall attract hate. It is only as we forgive that we can be forgiven. *Forgive us our debts, as we forgive our debtors* places immediate salvation within the reach of all, while, at the same time, showing that we shall suffer so long as we impose suffering. This is justice without judgment. This is a bold statement that mere protestations do not suffice. We must actually partake of the Divine Nature if we are to portray it. We must forgive if we are to be forgiven; we must love if we would be loved. This is the law of cause and effect. There is no escape from it.

We cannot expect the universe to make an exception for our individual case. It is only when we share that we possess. It is only when we seek the greatest good for all that we can hope to experience that good in our individual lives. As we feel close to God, so we must also feel close to everyone and everything, for God is all-in-all. Love alone liberates. There is no happy life without love. Forgiving everyone, including ourselves, releases us from tension and takes away all bitterness from the mind.

God holds nothing against us, therefore we need never worry about our relationship with Him. But in order that love may be fulfilled, we must lavishly expend it on others. It should not be difficult to learn to love the world, and what a joy to find the world loving us!

And lead us not into temptation, but deliver us from evil . . . This is not so much a supplication as it is a statement of spiritual conviction. The Spirit cannot lead us into temptation, therefore It must deliver us from evil, just as light delivers us from darkness. No matter what happened yesterday, today can give birth to the Kingdom of God in our experience.

For thine is the kingdom, and the power, and the glory, for ever. Amen. This kingdom, this power and this glory never change. The truth is forever established: eternal in its infancy, eternal in its maturity, it knows no decay. We must believe that the gift of life is already an accomplished fact. We must have faith that God will meet all our needs, right where we are.

The only limitation the law of life sets on us—and this is no limitation at all—is that each completes the circle of his own desire only in such degree as he is willing to share with others the good he wishes to receive. Could we ask for more, or could we in justice expect it to be otherwise? Giving and receiving; loving and being loved; helping and being helped; living and letting live—is not this the Kingdom of God?

CHAPTER VIII

The Word of Power

Jesus, the greatest spiritual genius of all time, said that our prayers should be prayers of faith: our meditations, contemplations of certainty. Our faith must reach beyond facts to that something which makes facts out of its own affirmation, creates form out of its own substance, and projects experience through the law of its own word.

He translated the universe in terms of mind and spirit. Man is one with the Spirit and one with the universal law of cause and effect. All things are possible to God, who creates through the power of His own divine imagination. The Divine Nature circulates through man, else he would have no life. Man's word is creative, not because he wills or wishes it, but because this is the nature of his being.

Our impulse to create comes from the original creative Spirit which is in, around and through us. The urge to live creatively comes from the urge of the Divine Imagination which pushes Itself out through us into self-expression. This is man's nature. He neither made it nor can he change it. He is compelled to live under its law.

There is a unifying and co-ordinating will in the universe whose nature is love and goodness. Therefore, Jesus carefully showed that when our thoughts are contrary to this divine goodness they must ultimately bring so much discomfort that we shall gladly renounce them for the pearl of great price, the unity of good. Using our thought constructively, thinking the thoughts of God after Him, we re-create our individual world more nearly after the divine pattern that the Spirit has already implanted within us.

Jesus, walking with the multitude, diffused a healing power which touched people into wholeness by its divine presence. His command stilled the wind and wave. His knowledge of spiritual law fed the thousands. His consciousness of peace calmed the troubled mind. His love was a healing balm to the sick. He possessed a transcendent power. He consciously brought this power to bear upon his environment. He told his followers that what he was doing they could do if they believed they could. The whole mystery and meaning of the teaching of Jesus is bound up in this word *believe*.

He so often talked about the more abundant life, the greater happiness, the deeper peace. He must have experienced uncertainty but unlike most of us, he triumphed. He walked over the waters of doubt, the waves of confusion and the tempests of unbelief. He was a happy and radiant soul. He was triumphant. His inward ear was in tune with the divine harmony; his inward eye looked upon a spiritual universe; his human consciousness was transmuted into divine understanding as he sought for and found unity with life.

He said very little about the negative conditions he wished to change. He took an opposite position. Instead of telling God how sick and poor people were, how famished and lonely they were, he affirmed the opposite. He told the lame to walk, the blind to see, the dumb to speak and the deaf to hear. He commanded the waves to be still, even while they were turbulently tossing around him. He was calm in the midst of the storm.

The Master assures us it is the Divine Will that we live abundantly, even while he warns that the use of the creative power of our thought must be constructive else we shall suffer the results of its destructive use. In this respect his teaching was similar to that of Moses who had said, "Behold, I set before you this day a blessing and a curse: A blessing, if ye obey the commandments . . . And a curse, if ye will not obey the commandments . . ." The average person sincerely desires to unify with the living Spirit. The necessary conditions that Jesus lays down for the good life are faith, belief and love.

Since belief and faith are mental attitudes, no external condition whatsoever can hinder us from thinking independently of our present circumstances and thereby creating a new set of situations more nearly molded after the heart's desire. To view the words of Jesus merely as symbols of divine ideals with no practical value would be so to dilute his teaching that it could mean nothing in this world other than a forlorn hope. But to understand, with him, that the Kingdom of God is at hand, that everything already exists in the divine potential, and to understand that today is eternity, is to realize that the Kingdom which is always at hand can be experienced here if we enter into it, imbibe its spirit, and live from its impulsion.

It was James, following Jesus, who said, "And the prayer of faith shall save the sick, and the Lord shall raise him up." This implies that spiritual power can be used for physical healing. Faith is the key to the use of this power. Faith itself is not the power but the way to use it.

If we try to make our faith work without the power we are merely holding thoughts, mentally trying to force things to happen. This would be a denial of the power. But when we see that faith is a way through which the power works we can approach it in calm confidence. It is the Lord who raises up the sick. It is Life that heals. Not our thought, not our will, not even our faith. But it is our faith that permits the power to flow through us.

Just as we set up a generator at a waterfall and capture natural energy to use for definite purposes, so we can set up an attitude of faith which catches a spiritual energy that is everywhere present. The generator does not put power into the waterfall, it takes it out. So it is with faith. We are surrounded by a creative force which operates upon our thinking but which is independent of our thoughts. It is upon this energy that we rely when we use faith. We provide a channel through which it flows.

How much of this power will flow through any particular prayer? As much as we believe in. Faith, belief, hope, expectancy and acceptance act as a measure. There is no question as to the volume of the power. The question is: how large is our measure; how much can we believe? The flow of the power will be an automatic reaction to our belief.

Jesus taught that the laws of nature can be likened to laws of thought. Every law of nature has a corresponding reality in the world of mind and spirit. To bring this down to a practical application, let us consider the law of circulation. Everything starts from a certain point and returns to it. The impulsion from the point at which anything starts is sufficient in its propulsion to cause it to return by a power inherent within itself. Therefore, Jesus was able to say that heaven and earth would pass away but his word would not until all become fulfilled. Faith on its circuit has a creative power within itself which can produce objective situations that outpicture such faith.

To the Man of Wisdom faith is not only a fact, it acts as law. It is this kind of faith he calls upon us to use. No one yet has disproved this magnificent claim that every soul may make upon the Mind of God. Faith should be used consciously and naturally and with no sense of confusion. As Paul said, "For if I pray in an unknown tongue, my spirit prayeth, but my understanding is unfruitful . . . I had rather speak five words with my understanding . . . than ten thousand words in an unknown tongue . . . For God is not the author of confusion, but of peace."

Paul understood the difference between spiritual illumination and psychic hallucination, between being led by the Spirit and controlled by subjective impulses. He knew that the intellect should be made an instrument of the Spirit. He knew that many of the prophecies given in the name of truth are but projections of unconscious desires. We need not become unconscious to be spiritual. Nothing that really emanates from the Spirit will confuse the intellect.

It would be impossible to understand the teaching of Jesus without realizing that he believed that the spiritual world presses around us. This spiritual universe contains the invisible patterns of everything on earth. The Greeks had taught this same philosophy and we find Paul saying, ". . . we look not at the things which are seen, but at the things which are not seen: for the things which are seen are temporal; but the things which are not seen are eternal."

The divine pattern or prototype is an eternal reality. Paul speaks of the visible as "our earthly house of this tabernacle," and of the eternal as "a building of God, an house not made with hands, eternal in the heavens." And he adds that we are "to be clothed upon with our house which is from heaven." When our thought is clothed upon by Spirit it takes on the nature of Spirit.

"For we walk by faith, not by sight" and ". . . if any man be in Christ, he is a new creature: old things are passed away; behold, all things are become new." Walking by faith, mentally feeling our way back to the Spirit, we become new creatures in Christ. To become a new creature in Christ means to become aware of one's intimate relationship with God. It is then that we are clothed upon by that Divine pattern which already exists, as though the mantle of our heavenly home descends upon the tabernacle of our earthly house.

We should, as the Apostle advises, "be strong in the Lord, and in the power of his might" and realize that "we wrestle not against flesh and blood but . . . against . . . the darkness," which he called spiritual wickedness. In this darkness is included everything that denies the nature and the supremacy of good. Paul tells us to put on "the whole armor of God . . . and having done all, to stand." This is a challenge to our spiritual conviction. It is also a challenge to our intellectual courage.

Faith, which is necessary to everyone's life, reaches back to the Source of being. In showing us how to arrive at this faith Paul says, "Stand therefore, having your loins girt about with truth, and having on the breastplate of righteousness; And your feet shod with the preparation of the gospel of peace." Faith is a shield against which the fiery darts of evil cannot prevail. It is a breastplate protecting the heart from hurt and the mind from doubt. The full armor of faith ties the intellect back to the heart of love from which no harm can come.

". . . take the helmet of salvation, and the sword of the Spirit, which is the word of God." The sword of Spirit which severs evil is the word of truth Jesus spoke of when he said, "Ye shall know the truth, and the truth shall make you free." There is a truth, the knowledge of which automatically brings freedom.

The word of truth is the sword of the Spirit against which nothing can prevail.

After explaining that we are joint heirs with Christ, Paul tells us the stroy of Abraham and his two sons, "the one by a bondmaid, the other by a freewoman," an allegory of two covenants, one which is made in bondage and the other which comes from freedom. He says that one "answereth to Jerusalem which now is, and is in bondage," but that the "Jerusalem which is above is free, which is the mother of us all."

We at once recognize this as a description of our divine state which exists in the Kingdom of God, and our earthly state which comes under the law of ignorance. In the fullness of time, Paul says, the Son of God came "to redeem them that were under the law," that we might receive the adoption of sons "wherefore thou art no more a servant but a son, and if a son, then an heir of God through Christ."

Paul, great mystic and spiritual philosopher, basing his thought on the teaching of Jesus, said that when we discover our true Father we shall pass from bondage into freedom. We shall no longer be subject to the law of ignorance but redeemed through knowing the truth. Thus the heavenly Jerusalem, "the mother of us all," hovers the earthly Jerusalem as a hen hovers her chickens.

In one of his letters to his followers Paul writes,

"My little children, of whom I travail in birth again until Christ be formed in you . . . Stand fast therefore in the liberty wherewith Christ hath made us free, and be not entangled again with the yoke of bondage." While we are the sons of earth only, we are in bondage to that which is earthly. When we recognize our sonship with God, Christ is formed in us. Though still on this earth, we need no longer be entangled in bondage.

This was the dynamic secret of Jesus. He had discovered the laws of Mind and Spirit which parallel physical laws and which, without destroying physical laws, transcend them. It was because of this knowledge that he had dominion over the physical world.

We need not deny the physical world, but rather, affirm a spiritual world transcendent of the physical, making the physical a servant of the spiritual. In our thinking we should theoretically transpose the physical into the spiritual, realizing that the spiritual controls the physical fact. This would be to stand fast in the liberty wherewith Christ has made us free.

"For we through the Spirit wait for the hope of righteousness by faith." Turning our mental gaze to the Spirit, through faith we can bring about any desired result which belongs to the Kingdom of Good. It is in this way that the just live by faith. ". . . if ye are led of the Spirit, ye are not under the law . . .

the fruit of the Spirit is love, joy, peace . . . goodness, faith . . . against such there is no law."

It is not for nothing that both Jesus and Paul demand a surrender of the isolated self to an all-inclusive love we should have for God, for one another
and for all creation. Love alone makes the complete
surrender because love alone sees itself in the other
and the other in itself. It is this love of, or in,
Christ that Paul says "passeth knowledge, that he
might be filled with all the fulness of God . . . according to the power that worketh in us." The
power that works in us is the Spirit of Life Itself.

There is a law of correspondences in nature. For
every external fact there is an inner thought pattern which exactly corresponds to it. This is why
Jesus said when we pray we should believe we already have received what we ask for.

In this way we are thinking in terms of an absolute
power and not in terms of a relative power. We are
planting a seed in the Mind of the Absolute which
must bear fruit. We are creating a nucleus which, as
soon as it is created, exercises an attractive force,
drawing to it everything necessary for its own accomplishment. Our thought of anything creates a spiritual prototype of that thing. Within this prototype
there is a law of growth which ever tends to produce the desired result.

We do not have to know the specific means by

which our good is coming to us. We must be sure and never doubt that this good is forthcoming. Our intellect may become a great hindrance or a great help. If it causes doubt it is a hindrance. If, on the other hand, it reasons these things through and comes to the conclusion of their reality, it is a great help.

The Universal Mind responds to us by corresponding with our mental approach to It. If our approach is constructive, only good can result. The slightest element of destructiveness, however, will bring a corresponding reaction. This is not because of any theological anathema, but because of the law of cause and effect with which we are dealing.

Jesus spent no time in mortifying the flesh. He did not live a life of solitary exclusion. The methods that many Eastern teachers practiced he brushed aside, proclaiming that the Kingdom of God, which includes everything, is at hand. He viewed the world of effect as something cast upon the screen of experience by internal causes which project it, and he knew these causes to be spiritual and unified at the base.

He did not teach that after untold years of renunciation we shall finally find peace. Rather, he said, in effect: "You are in the midst of peace now. Lay aside your confusion and you will find that peace is already here. It was here all the time." What Jesus did, which other leaders failed to do in so great a degree, was to unite life with living, heaven with earth, and God with man. Heaven, to him, was not something to gain but something to become aware of.

It was this complete simplicity, this direct approach, which his contemporaries could not understand. They were used to the physical austerities practiced by those who sought spiritual enlightenment or the intellectual attainments of those trained in the art of argument. When one came who joyously proclaimed that the Kingdom was at hand and theirs for the taking, they could not comprehend such a simple approach.

It is just as difficult for us to comprehend it today. We, too, have our shibboleths, our dogmas, our systems. They are so unintegrated, so divided against themselves, so far away from the simple truth Jesus proclaimed. Why is it so difficult for us to follow his simple method? The answer lies in a vast system of false spiritual education—not false in the sense that it is insincere but false because it is largely built on a wrong premise. For most theology is based on the theory that man is separated from God.

The Wise One by-passed all this and said, in essence: "Come with me into the fields. Come out in the desert. Sit by the shores of the lake. The table is already spread. Eat! Be not afraid, only believe!" Jesus believed in a spiritual power which responded to his faith. And he said that all may use this power.

He said this spiritual power responds to our be-

lief in it. This means that we should have specific
desires in mind if we wish our faith to be rewarded.
Faith is a mental attitude which no longer permits
itself to conceive of an opposite. It is more than a
hopeful mental attitude or an expectant affirmation.
It is an attitude of mind that completely accepts the
result even though, objectively, it does not see it.
This is why Jesus tells us to judge not according to
appearances but to look behind the appearance and
believe in a power which can change the old experience and produce a new one.

No doubt this is one of the difficult things to follow
in the teaching of Jesus. No one could do this unless,
following the instruction of the Great Master, he was
able to convince thimself that there is a power greater
than he is, greater than anything that is happening
to him. This power is not limited to situations as
they now are because it can project new circumstances and new conditions.

When we examine our mental reactions and realize how difficult it is to bring them to a place of complete belief, we better understand what Jesus was
trying to teach us. For we, too, are his disciples. He
was the Master Mind of the ages and his life points a
way to the use of Divine Power such as no other person before or since has set before the mind of man.
But remembering that Jesus was the great example
and not the great exception, we should realize that

his teaching will remain merely a divine symphony played nearly two thousand years ago unless we tune our own instrument to that harmony which was his.

Lest the greatest of all examples become a forlorn hope or a forgotten memory, we, too, must follow his teaching, not only with admiration and gratitude, but equally with a determination to make those thoughts and words which were real to him, real to us.

It is impossible to read the words of this illumined soul without realizing that his mission was based on the concept that what he did others could do also. He has laid down the rules. He has given us the formulas. He has shown us the way. But even he cannot walk that way for us. We, too, must start at humble beginnings, take such faith as we now possess, and build on it until finally there comes the triumph of the Spirit, the supremacy of good, the all-conquering power of love.

The use of the law of good Jesus set down in the simple word *belief*. But our mental household is divided against itself. In one moment we believe and in the next we doubt. It frequently seems as though fear and faith are almost equal opposites. But experience teaches us that we can conquer fear with faith, even as we can overcome darkness with light. "For the light shineth in the darkness, and the darkness comprehendeth it not," that is, the darkness has no power over it.

When the Master said, "It is done unto you as you believe," he was stating the crux of the whole matter. Our belief is a medium between the invisible cause and the manifestation of that cause through us. One side of the mind listens to the Spirit. The other side looks at externals. When the side that listens to the Spirit dominates, our thoughts are of faith in that which is greater than we are, in that which has the power of life itself.

The intellect is mostly caught in the stream of conditions of everyday living. It is taking its images of thought from effects rather than causes. Therefore, it perpetuates the very effects from which it seeks to free itself. And according to the law of cause and effect, fear brings to us the condition that faith could dissipate. This is not because we are dealing with duality, but with a unity so complete, so perfect, so exact, that individual freedom must bear the responsibility of choice until experience teaches us how to choose wisely and well.

This is the great teaching of the Wayshower relative to the law of good which all may use. The complete simplicity, the directness of his approach, has confounded humanity. When they brought him a man possessed with evil whom his disciples had been

unable to heal, the one who had risen above all confusion had no difficulty in dissipating that evil. His
disciples had done the best they could, but their best
was not sufficient.

There was no effort on his part when he healed
this man. He merely saw him in the light of Spirit.
His disciples had seen him in the light of confusion.
Jesus was at home in the life of the Spirit. They
were almost strangers to it.

And now, after nearly two thousand years, we also
come to the humble beginning of our search after
that consciousness which Jesus so completely em-
bodied. It is certain that we must start where we
are. Any journey must start from the point where
we are to the point we desire to reach. The shortest
distance between two points is a straight line. The
shortest distance between our confusion and the consciousness of Christ is resolutely to lay down that confusion and commune with the Spirit until confusion
has left us.

We should not be discouraged if our first efforts
are weak and feeble in the light of our high hope.
Patiently we must work with ourselves until we learn
to live by an all-conquering faith which, coupled
with love, is the highest law of life and the greatest
gift of heaven.

The Great Teacher never asked the impossible.
He understood our human frailties and had compas-

sion for our shortcomings. But he knew that until fear and confusion are converted into faith and confidence they will continue to produce their logical results. Jesus was the most completely logical man who ever lived. He combined logic, faith and reason with spiritual awareness and discovered and lived in a spiritual universe, here and now.

Why is it so difficult for us to have faith? The answer is simple enough. We are so weighted with experiences that contradict faith. It is not easy to turn from negative conditions to a positive faith in God. Carefully we should cultivate the smallest spark of faith and we should always be reminding ourselves that there is a power upon which we may rely. We must throw ourselves with complete abandonment into this power, for it will never fail us.

On one occasion his disciples came to Jesus complaining that certain people who were not his followers were casting out devils in his name. They told their master they had forbidden them to do this. His answer was exactly what we should expect: "Forbid them not, for he that is not against us is on our part." Here we find him cutting a straight line through theological controversy and dogmatic practices. He knew that Divine Power responds to everyone.

We need not wonder if the words of our prayers are correct, only if they are sincere. We need not ask what form of worship is acceptable to the Spirit, merely, are we drawing closer to Divine Love? We need not ask, will the law of life respond to our approach? but only, are we having faith? We need not ask, will Divine Love reward us for our good works? but, are we thinking only in the terms of Divine Love? We need not ask, does our intellect comprehend the meaning of life? only, are we sincerely following the teaching of the Master? Have we humbled our spiritual pride and intellectual arrogance? Have we sought the Kingdom as a child?

Again let us remember the two fundamental principles on which the entire teaching of Jesus was based —the understanding of the universe as a combination of love and law, of person and principle, of feeling and force. Is it difficult to conceive of infinite incorporeal person, the essence of our personal being?

Biology is the science of life, yet it fails to explain what or why life is. Psychology is the science of mental and emotional actions and reactions, yet it fails to explain what or why the mind is. Philosophy is an investigation into the nature of a reality which it can only feel but never see, nor can it explain what or why this reality is. Religion deals with the relationship between God and man, yet no one has ever seen God.

It is not necessary that we grasp the full significance of infinite Presence. It is necessary that we believe in a universal Love and Beauty and an Intelligence which responds to us. It was this Divine Spirit with which Jesus communed, drawing from It inspiration such as no other man has ever received, such power as no other man, before or since, has had.

It is self-evident that if one wishes to resolve conflicts in his mind he must first reach a place where there is no conflict, that the lesser become absorbed in the greater, the little lost in the all. If we wish to follow the teaching of the Blessed One and make it practical we must endeavor to reach an elevation of consciousness where conflict ceases and true communion begins. For there can be no real spiritual communion until conflict ceases. We must surrender confusion if we would find peace.

Perhaps we have misinterpreted the meaning of this submission, the necessity of which Jesus clearly taught. Possibly we are afraid lest we become absorbed in something so much greater than we are that we lose all personal sense of being. Tagore has beautifully told us that Nirvana is not absorption but immersion. Jesus, with greater profoundness, has told us that in losing our lives we shall find them.

We need not lose our personal sense of being but should discover it in a universal unity from which good alone can flow. Rather, then, than losing our lives we shall truly find them. We shall find that our intellectual and emotional capacities become deepened and sharpened through conscious communion with the Spirit. It was from this communion that Jesus received the inspiration to speak those words which not only moved men's minds but with equal power healed their bodies.

Suppose we entertain the idea that there is a Divine Intelligence operating through everything in accord with the law of Its own being; that every objective fact in nature must have an equal but invisible subjective cause. If the universe is the effect of Divine Intelligence operating as law, then the movement of this Intelligence, in and upon Itself, must automatically project a manifestation which is identical with such inward movement or imagination.

"In the beginning was the Word, and the Word was with God, and the Word was God . . . All things were made by him; and without him was not any thing made that was made." This statement, with which we are all so familiar, is simple enough from a superficial viewpoint, but considering it as an actual statement of a law of cause and effect, no such an interpretation would be adequate.

Nothing is more certain than that Life is. While we do not know the exact nature of this Life, and neither science, philosophy nor religion has penetrated very far beneath the veil of our objective world, it is certain that this world which we experience must have an unseen and intelligent cause that holds it in place through the law of its own being. Since we find certain located activities or manifestations of Life, we cannot fail to concede that whatever the nature of this Divine Intelligence may be, It has volition as well as imagination.

We cannot escape the conclusion that creation is the manifestation of an infinite Intelligence operating through selectivity and will, bringing conscious means to definite ends. We are one of these ends. The greatest thinkers of the ages have concluded that there is a Divine Pattern or Prototype back of, or within, each form. All the holy books, scriptures and bibles of the ages have started with the simple proposition that a universal creative agency, thinking, knowing and willing within itself, creates patterns or types, which, in their turn, through the action of law, produce manifest forms or effects that are identical with the pattern or prototype back of, or within, them.

In studying our own nature we discover that the fundamental reality within us is the ability to think, to know, to imagine and to will. There can be no experience without consciousness. Consciousness is the one solid, final and fundamental basis upon which all speculation about the nature of Life must be built, for without consciousness there can be nothing with which to speculate.

In studying our consciousness we discover the intimate relationship between our mental life and our physical body, between our modes of thought and what happens to us. The pattern is not yet completely worked out, but enough has been ascertained to justify us in the assurance that without consciousness, so far as we are concerned, there could be no existence. No doubt, if we could completely penetrate our own nature, we should discover that mysterious essence of life which is cryptic in everything. The next great discovery of science will be in the realm of the human psyche.

Throughout the ages there have been those, who, by some interior awareness, have come to the conclusion that man is an individualized center in a Universal Mind in which all things are rooted; that this Universal Mind is self-existent, self-sustaining, self-animating and self-projective.

It is evident that this universal will and imagination must be creative and that it can never be divided against itself. The Spirit must be one, unified in intent, purpose and execution. Therefore, the Spirit is infinite harmony. It is equally necessary that It be infinite givingness, for only through the act of giving Itself to Its creation could It find fulfillment or self-realization. Thus we find that God is harmony, God is love, God is unity, God is law, God is givingness.

Since the Divine Mind knows nothing outside Itself, different from or opposed to Its own inward harmony, It must forever remain in infinite peace, and since the Divine Spirit cannot help coming to fruition through Its own act, It must be infinite completion, happiness and joy. Since It is the original creative artist operating from peace, harmony and joy, It must be eternal contentment. This is why Emerson tells us that the Infinite "lies stretched in smiling repose."

Jesus called this Infinite Intelligence "our Father which art in heaven." He located heaven within as well as around us. To him, God was both an indwelling and an overshadowing Presence. Like other great mystics he believed that the "highest God and the innermost God is one God." It was with this Divine Presence in people and in nature that he communed. To him It must have seemed a warm, colorful, responsive and intelligent Presence.

"There is one body, and one Spirit . . . One God and Father of all, who is above all, and through all, and in you all," said Paul. It is difficult for the intellect to follow this all-inclusive idea of unity. It is difficult to realize that there is but one body. With greater ease we conceive the meaning of one Spirit. If there is but one Spirit every form must be some part of the body of this Spirit. This includes our physical bodies which must have a divine prototype in the spiritual world.

Should we discover this spiritual pattern within, and the mind completely accept it, our physical diseases would drop away because they are not included in the divine pattern. It is in turning from the body to the Spirit, which is one with both body and mind, that we receive a divine influx that heals the flesh. "From whom the whole body fitly joined together . . . according to the effectual working in the measure of every part, maketh increase of the body . . . that ye put off . . . the old man . . . And be renewed in the spirit of your mind." It is this renewal of the mind in the Spirit which permits the flow of Spirit into our bodies and affairs. It could not be otherwise.

The divine prototypes already exist in the Spirit. When the mind is open to these spiritual patterns they are let down, as it were, into the flesh or into the body of our affairs. Therefore, the mind must be brought into subjection to the Spirit. This is what Paul meant when he said, ". . . he led captivity captive . . . Till we all come in the unity of the faith, and of the knowledge of the Son of God, unto a perfect man, unto the measure of the stature of the fulness of Christ." When the mind is brought into subjection to the Spirit the chains of bondage fall apart.

"Now that he ascended, what is it but that he also descended . . . He that descended is the same also that ascended . . . that he might fill all things." Paul is presenting the picture of a complete union between heaven and earth, between the Spirit, which is the cause, and creation, which is its effect. As there is one Spirit, one Cause, so there is one creation, one effect. It is this Cause which descends into creation while creation is lifted back again into its cause that the two may be one "which after God is created in righteousness and true holiness."

Jesus viewed the universe as a spiritual system— one, undivided and indivisible unit. He thought of God as the heavenly Father, immediately personal to all, and the word of God as the Divine Nature manifesting Itself as law. He thought of man as being in immediate relationship to this Divine Life.

His entire philosophy was based on the concept that Divine Love and Law are everywhere present. They are available to all who comply with their nature. Complying with the law of love is what he called "knowing the truth." It was a knowledge of this truth that enabled Jesus to perform those wonderful acts which his age, and the ages since, have looked upon as miracles.

This illumined soul came not to destroy but to fulfill, not to tear down but to build up. His message was one of healing and comfort, of love and compassion. He viewed those around him as little children in faith and built upon the best they knew. It is no wonder they marveled at the brilliancy and depth of his teaching; no wonder they stood in awe before his spiritual illumination.

And now, with the Great Master, we must view the universe as a spiritual system. This system includes ourselves and all nature. We must reinterpret the universe in terms of an infinite Thinker. It is God knowing Himself in form. We are some part of the divine self-knowingness of the Spirit. Its creativeness is in our consciousness, making it necessary that we live, not from without alone, but also from within. As God is in the universal, so man is in the individual. As God works, so man works. This was the great truth Jesus proclaimed. This was the secret of his power.

CHAPTER IX

Healing Miracles

AND ". . . they followed him on foot out of the cities . . ." and ". . . he was moved with compassion toward them, and he healed their sick." Always Jesus was moved with compassion by human distress. Having bathed in the ocean of wholeness it was his desire to share this wholeness with others.

In this healing ministry a centurion came to him, beseeching him to heal his servant. And Jesus said, "I will come and heal him." The answer of the centurion is worthy of our consideration: ". . . speak the word only, and my servant shall be healed." He recognized an authority in the Master that he likened to his own authority.

He said that he was a man who had servants and soldiers under him and if he said to one, "Come!" he would come, or to another, "Go!" he would go, or to a third, "Do this, and he doeth it." Being a man of authority he had a mental equivalent of the authority Jesus exercised on an invisible plane. The centurion recognized that his authority was in his word, to which some law responded, always honoring that word. His answer seemed to delight Jesus, who said, "I have not found so great faith, no not in Israel. Go thy way, and as thou hast believed so be it done unto thee."

In this simple statement which healed the centurion's servant, at the very moment it was spoken, lies one of the deepest mysteries of life. It is not only done unto us *because* we believe, it is done unto us *as* we believe. There is something that responds to us by corresponding with our faith in it. In its stark nakedness the teaching is so simple that we can easily overlook its meaning and the possibility it suggests.

Jesus had implicit faith in an everpresent Power whose rule is absolute and whose law is perfect. His will and imagination were completely abandoned to this conviction. What years of sincere seeking must have preceded the culmination of his search! What waiting and longing, what sorrow and rejoicing! What pathways of self-discipline he must have followed we know not. But we can well imagine that the spiritual height he had reached was not gained in a brief period of time. It must have taken years to come to such a complete abandonment to that truth that never failed him. Its bare simplicity staggers our imagination even as its implication stimulates our hope.

We are all searching for this pearl of great price. Why have so few found it? Could the answer be because we have sought it outside the self? Are we not seeking too much in externals, weighing this against that and that against something else? *It is done unto you as you believe* is one of the simplest statements the Great One made. It should be a hope to which we may cling, a shelter in the time of storm, a great light in darkness.

There is that which we must believe; there is also much that we must surrender. This is shown in the incident of a disciple who said he wished to follow the Master but first he would like to bury his father. The answer was a symbol of much that impedes progress for Jesus said, "Let the dead bury their dead." We cannot live in our tomorrows or in our yesterdays. The mistakes, fears and doubts of yesterday we need not bury. They will liquidate themselves when they no longer find nourishment in today. That which we refuse to feed shrivels up and dies.

Always we shall remember the occasion when multitudes followed Jesus out of the city into a desert place. Evening had come and his disciples besought him to send them away ". . . that they may go into the villages and buy themselves victuals." His reply must have surprised them: "They need not depart; give ye them to eat."

His astonished followers said, "We have here but five loaves, and two fishes." Little did they know they were about to behold an act of faith which actually precipitated substance in the form of loaves and fishes. Taking the five loaves and two fishes, and looking up, Jesus blessed them and they were multiplied. He gave them to his disciples and the multitude was fed.

"And looking up, he blessed the loaves and fishes." What was this spiritual genius looking up to other than the spiritual substance which evermore surrounds us? If he had looked down he would have seen but a few loaves and a few small fish. He would have seen thousands of people physically hungry, weary with the day's journey, exhausted by the heat and the excited enthusiasm of the occasion. What would a few loaves and a few fish be among so many? But Jesus did not look down. He looked up. He did not curse the meagre fare spread before him. He merely took it as a pattern of abundance. He blessed the substance, gave thanks for the increase, and let the Lord of the harvest multiply his seed of faith.

After the thousands had been fed such an abundance was left over that many baskets were required to carry it away. God's givingness is neither meagre

nor limited. As the Wise One said on another occasion, "good measure, well shaken down, and running over" shall the Spirit give into the hands of
uplifted belief.

We should learn to bless what we have, to give
thanks for what we see. What blessings we miss
through our lack of faith! Have we really practiced
faith with the same enthusiasm that we put into other
things? Have we practiced becoming aware of good
in the midst of evil? Have we practiced peace instead
of confusion? How many of us are affirmative in
everyday language? It seems as though we deliberately practice denials instead of affirmations. Not
only do we refuse to believe in the givingness of God,
we deny it almost continuously.

After the multitude was fed Jesus told his disciples
to go into a ship and depart for the other side of
the lake while he went up into a mountain to pray.
He went alone. This is the story of everyone's life.
Spiritual awareness is of the "alone to the alone," of
the "one to the one." There is a mountain within
each of us, God's holy mountain. The ascent into
this mountain must be made alone because no one
can live for us.

While the Master was praying his disciples had
taken ship for the other side of the lake and their
"ship was out in the midst of the sea, tossed with
waves." They were unable to make headway be-

cause "the wind was contrary," and looking up they saw Jesus walking on the water. Their first reaction was that they were seeing a ghost. But he said to them, "Be of good cheer; it is I; be not afraid." He must have deliberately waited until the waves were about to submerge the boat before he came to their rescue.

The Great Teacher was always showing his followers how to meet even the most trivial difficulties. He never condemned the use of spiritual power for personal purposes. He taught that everything is subject to spiritual power. Why should not Spirit be able to control the wind and waves of human experience?

Jesus did not teach a mitigation of evil. He taught the overcoming of evil with good. He did not teach that God gives us strength to withstand wind and wave. He taught that God controls wind and wave. His was no metaphorical teaching only. It was a direct and conscious application of spiritual power to human needs.

The impetuous Peter, who loved his master so dearly, seeing him walking over the waves asked him to bid him come to him. The first enthusiastic thought of Peter was a complete abandonment to faith. He was looking at Jesus and not the waves. Therefore, he eagerly started to walk over the water, "but when he saw the wind boisterous, he was afraid;

and beginning to sink, he cried, saying, Lord, save me!" And "Jesus stretched forth his hand, and caught him, and said unto him, O thou of little faith, wherefore doest thou doubt?"

What a lesson for all of us! We are buoyed up by a little faith only to become submerged in doubt. We shout with joy at one moment and cry out in anguish at the next. However, it is futile to condemn ourselves for this because we must learn to take ourselves for better or for worse. We must start right where we are and build upon such hope and faith as we have.

It is well to cherish even a small amount of faith for it can lead us to a place where we may walk, not through, but over, the waves. It is this walking over the waves and not through them that we should remember. It is a looking up and not down; the replacing of fear with faith; confidence annulling our doubt; hope transmuting despair into courage. Christ forever comes to us over the troubled seas of human experience. The Divine Hand is always outstretched and love never faileth.

When Jesus commanded the wind and the wave to be still, the wind ceased and immediately the boat was at the shore. Is it too much to believe that the spiritual power of this emancipated soul could bring the boat immediately to the shore? Not if we believe that all things are possible to God. Not if we believe that Jesus understood the power of God. Why should not our boat be brought immediately to the shore? The present moment is as much a part of eternity as any future state can possibly become. The future is but the lengthened shadow of now and tomorrow will be today when it arrives.

Again multitudes came to the Great Physician beseeching him to heal them. Their faith was so great that they felt if they could but touch the hem of his garment they would be healed, ". . . and as many as touched were made perfectly whole." The garment of Jesus was made of one piece of cloth, cut in circular form, symbolizing the unity and wholeness of all life. Wholeness needs but to be touched to transmit its life-giving power to that which seems separated, to that which appears divided.

When one is filled with faith it may be transmitted to others. When one is filled with light he helps to lighten the pathway for others. When one has a consciousness of the Divine Presence others feel this Presence and enter into Its light with him. God grant that we, too, may don the seamless robe of truth and, as the Apostle so beautifully said, be clothed upon from heaven.

And as Jesus walked about two blind men followed him, crying out that he have mercy on them and heal them. As he so often did, he asked if they believed he could do this and when they answered, "Yes," he touched their eyes and restored their sight. He told them to tell no one what had happened.

It seems probable that their faith was not very deeply rooted but that they were caught up in the excitement and enthusiasm of the moment. They were, in a sense, enveloped in a field of faith generated by those around them. Realizing this, Jesus told them not to talk about their healing. It was necessary for them to become established in their own faith lest their unconscious doubts mingle with the unbelief of others and cause them to return to the old condition.

In moments of great enthusiasm hope may temporarily outweigh despair and faith produce a temporary manifestation. But faith must become subjective, it must be inwardly established before it can be permanent. The whole unconscious expectation must be transmuted from fear into faith. This explains why many of our prayers seem to be answered only for a while. We have not yet built up a faith that cannot be shaken. We must have the patience and perseverance to carry through to the day of lasting victory.

One of the greatest lessons of the Great Teacher was the healing of the man "possessed with a devil." "As they went out, behold, they brought to him a dumb man possessed with a devil," and Jesus rebuked the evil spirit and it came out of him and the man was restored to sanity. Whether we think of the evil spirit as an actual obsession or as an obsession of one's own thought, makes no difference. Probably the man was suffering from some form of insanity. Jesus never seemed to be concerned over the why and what of people's troubles because he knew of a larger why and what.

The scribes murmured among themselves, saying that Jesus cast out devils by the power of evil itself. But this man of inspiration, who was also a man of logic, said that if he used evil to cast out evil then would "Satan rise up against himself and be divided; he cannot stand, but hath an end." But, he added, if he cast out evil with the power of good, then "the Kingdom of Heaven is come among you." He was announcing a self-evident proposition: good alone overcomes evil, right alone destroys wrong, only peace and faith can supplant fear and doubt.

In another instance they brought to Jesus a man blind from his birth. Hoping to catch him in an impossible position, they asked whether the man were born blind because of previous mistakes or because of the sins of his parents. In that day there was a division of opinion as to whether people suffered through the sins of previous incarnations or by the misdeeds of their parents. Probably they reasoned with themselves, saying, "Since one or the other of these propositions must be true, Jesus will have to affirm one and deny the other."

However, the subtlety of their thought was no

match for the clarity of his. He utterly disregarded their questioning, as though he were saying, "What difference does it make? The power of God is sufficient to overcome all mistakes." He knew it made no difference at what point of time the mistake was made. What matters is the point of time in which it is corrected. And so he healed the man. He did not argue about the man's sin or his parents' mistakes. He held no discourse over the theory of reincarnation or the influence of others. He knew the soul to be free, now.

Jesus never piled up the liabilities of yesterday against the possibilities of tomorrow, sandwiching today between two impossible situations, taking the daily bread from the mouth of need and giving us a moldy crust from yesterday or the forlorn hope for a crop not yet harvested. To this glorious soul each day is God's day. Forever fresh and eternally new is the springtime of our being.

But seldom do we enter into the joy of the moment in which we live. Too often it is overshadowed by the memories of yesterday or submerged in the futility of tomorrow's hope. The shadow of what was, and what is to be, clouds our minds, making it impossible for Divine Love to warm our hearts with that eternal light which neither increases nor diminishes.

It is evident that Jesus did not accept the theology of his day. So much that he taught was contradictory to the then, and the now, accepted beliefs. For he taught that the Kingdom of God is at hand, not something that is going to transpire, but something that is taking place now. Like Plato he taught that Divine Patterns of perfection exist in the Mind of God, and because the Mind of God is present everywhere, they exist at the center of our own being.

His teaching was based on the concept that man has a spiritual life, here and now; that the power of good is available, here and now. He definitely taught that we cannot use the higher law of our being until we seek a complete union with God, with love, with wisdom, and with righteousness. We see, then, that while his teaching is one of the utmost simplicity, it is, at the same time, the most profound teaching ever given the world. Both its simplicity and its profoundness have eluded us, just as life itself seems to in so many ways.

For instance, we all look for more life, not realizing that we already are living in all the life there is or can be. It was his teaching that the Kingdom of God is at hand; that we need no longer go in search after God, but rather, awake to a consciousness that the Divine already is. We are immersed in It, we are one with It, we are of It and from It. Jesus taught that love opens the doorway to the Kingdom, for God is love.

Paul also tells us that love does not rejoice in iniquity but in truth. Believing in truth, hoping for truth, it "endureth all things" until truth is established. Love never fails. Prophecies will fail, tongues will cease, human knowledge will "vanish away," for now "we know in part." Like Jesus, the Apostle believed in the divine patterns but knew we do not see them clearly. After saying that we know in part and prophesy in part, he adds, "But when that which is perfect is come, then that which is in part shall be done away." Paul did not argue as to whether or not the divine patterns exist. He took it for granted that they do.

Now we see in part and know in part, but gradually, as we put these parts together, we find a cosmic pattern likened to the new Jerusalem which is let down from heaven. When the perfect arrives the part will be done away with. Paul refers to our present state of evolution as though we were children. But "when I became a man I put away childish things."

Many of our beliefs will some day disappear. Much of our religions, philosophies, sciences and modes of human conduct will some day pass into oblivion. Not that they are evil. They are incomplete. "For now we see through a glass, darkly; but then face to face: now I know in part; but then shall I know even as also I am known."

The spiritual universe is here but we see it as though we were looking through dark glasses. We but half-interpret it. The spiritual outlines are lost in fear, superstition and unbelief. Yet, we do feel the something more that should be added. There is a voice forever telling us about this more—our interior awareness through which we enter the temple gates although we do not quite reach the Holy of Holies. Though now we see as through a glass, darkly, "then face to face . . . then shall I know even as also I am known." God knows us as we really are. When we shall know ourselves as God knows us, then what God knows about us will descend into us. Then shall we know as we are known.

We do not experience the fullness of life because we do not appreciate its meaning nor understand the law of its action. To the pure all is pure; to the good all is good; to the heavenly-minded all is heaven; to the God-inclined the God-ordained comes. The divine light is obstructed because we stand with our face turned from it.

Jesus said, "I am the light of the world," and, "Ye are the light of the world;" also, "Whoever committeth sin is the servant of sin. And the servant abideth not in the house forever, but the son abideth ever. If the son, therefore, shall make you free, ye shall be free indeed." In saying that whoever commits sin is a servant of sin but the servant abides not forever, he meant that the night of human ignorance must finally vanish in a morning of spiritual enlightenment. Sin, darkness and the night are temporary. They cannot abide in the house of God forever, but the son does abide forever. Good will finally come to all.

On one of his journeys a woman of Canaan came to Jesus beseeching him to heal her daughter who was vexed with a devil. He did not immediately answer her and again she besought his help. Turning to her he said, "It is not mete to take the children's bread and to cast it to dogs." The woman's reply was as keen as his own, for she said that even dogs eat crumbs from their master's table. Because her reply was so filled with meaning he answered, "O woman, great is thy faith. Be it unto thee even as thou wilt," and her daughter was instantly healed.

It seems as though Jesus were waiting for the woman's faith and acceptance to become a conveyor of his word of power. He knew that faith acts as law and that if the result is to be perfect the faith must be complete. He was testing the woman's belief. Seeing her faith rise to complete acceptance, he knew the moment had come to speak the word of power that would restore her daughter to sanity.

The Great Wayshower laid down every rule and method of procedure necessary for the right use of the law. There were thousands of prophets before him. In many cases they had taught intricate systems and complicated methods. People had become confused over these varying systems, with a law for this and a law for that and a law for something else; over the posture they were to assume in prayer, the different ways of fasting and feasting, the control of the breath, the discipline of the mind, the need to repudiate the entire objective world as though it were an illusion.

These systems were so complicated that the ordinary person could not understand, much less follow, them. It was the great spiritual genius of Jesus to reduce all of them to their common denominator and find the simple, affirmative factor running through all which gave reality and power to any. This is why he so carefully explained that it is not the method but the state of consciousness which the method leads to. The substance and essence of all these systems he proclaimed to be faith, conviction, trust—"It is done unto you as you believe."

When he said it is done unto you as you believe he must have implied *everything* we believe. Not only our spiritual awareness but everything that thought dwells on—our bodily health, our physical environment, our relationship with people, our communion with God. Jesus had such a profound concept of this that his thought, resting upon any person or object, instantly laid bare the inward nature of that person or object. He lifted his environment up rather than being dragged down by it. This was the triumph of his spiritual consciousness.

He lay no exclusive claim to the spiritual power he used. Rather, he told others that they possessed the same power. The power he used is available to all, and, according to Jesus, will respond to anyone who believes in it. "It is the spirit that quickeneth; the flesh profiteth· nothing: the words that I speak unto you, they are spirit, and they are life." It is only as the Spirit animates the flesh that the flesh takes on a livingness which reflects the Divine Life.

If we follow his teaching we shall discover the spiritual laws which govern the power he used. But he tells us that no man can do this of himself for "he that speaketh of himself seeketh his own glory." The spiritual power the Master commanded was his because he had completely unified himself with the Divine Presence.

Spiritual things are spiritually discerned. It would be impossible for anyone logically to deny the teaching of Jesus or its effects in human experience until he had first subjected himself to the rules which he laid down. There are on earth today a large number of persons who are sincerely and earnestly seeking to better understand the viewpoint of this most remarkable of all men. These people are not only sincere and earnest, they are extremely intelligent. There is a growing evidence of their inward conviction through actual signs that are following their belief.

It is impossible to escape this. They are the greatest hope on earth today.

"Then said Jesus unto them, When ye have lifted up the son of man, then shall ye know that I am he, and that I do nothing of myself, but as my Father hath taught me . . ." In this passage he tells us that the son of man is also the Son of God. When we lift up the son of man to his divine stature we shall see that the life of the son is also the life of the Father. However, the son can do nothing of himself alone, but only as the Father shows him.

The electric globe is not a light until the current passes through it. It cannot be a light of itself. It is an instrument through which the current flows. This also is true of the circuit of the Divine Mind through us. It too is a creative energy. Indeed, it is the ultimate energy as well as the ultimate intelligence. It is only as we live in harmony with the Divine Nature that there can be a free flow of Its intelligence and energy through us.

It is because of the possibility of this flow that the Man of Wisdom said, "If ye continue in my word, then are ye my disciples indeed, and ye shall know the truth, and the truth shall make you free." These words imply a spiritual power which is available to all. There can be no question of the implication of the meaning of the words. They are among the most profound utterances of this man whose intellect had penetrated the mystery of life and discovered the spiritual laws which govern everything.

The hope that should nestle like a conviction of certainty at the center of our being is a complete faith in the triumph of Spirit. Jesus healed the multitudes, not by power or by might, but through a surrender of human weakness to spiritual strength.

CHAPTER X

The Great Example

"VERILY I say unto you, The son can do nothing of himself, but . . . the Father loveth the son . . . and hath given him authority and showeth him all things that himself doeth, and . . . as the Father raiseth up the dead and quickeneth them, even so the son quickeneth whom he will." In these sentences Jesus announces one of the greatest of all spiritual truths. The living Spirit is incarnated in every man's soul; the entire nature of the Divine Being is bequeathed to us; there is a law of spiritual authority which is at our command.

Yet the Supreme Master was careful to say that we are not God, even though we are of like nature with Him. The son can do nothing of himself while he remains separated from the source of his being. But when he turns his whole thought and attention to the Divine, the life of God pouring through his being endows him with creativeness. Thus what the son sees the Father do, that the son does also.

Nor did Jesus place any limit upon our use of divine power. Rather, he said, in essence: Watch what I do, understand the words I speak, enter into conscious union with the Spirit, and you will do greater things than I have done. Surely, no other man ever issued such an invitation. Is it too much to believe that even war, pestilence and famine, poverty, unhappiness and disease might pass from the face of the earth if there were enough people who actually believed in and understood the teaching of Jesus, and followed it?

The skeptic may smile at this. The materialist may repudiate it. The intellect may not grasp its meaning. Most human experience may have contradicted it. And yet, standing clear against the horizon of human experience there was a man who faced the unbelief of the ages and made good his claim on God.

Jesus was either the great exception or the great example. If he were the great exception, there is little we can do other than admire the spiritual altitude from which he spoke. If he were the great example, we should follow his teaching and seek to make it practical in our everyday living. He chose to think of himself as the great example, saying that what he did we too can do if we follow the same rules, if we believe in God and have faith.

We shall not understand his teaching unless we keep in mind that he was placing himself in a relationship toward God that all men should assume. He was demonstrating to those of his day, and to those of our day, that there is a spiritual power which we may use. In no way did he intimate that God gave him a power that is withheld from others. He said, what I do shall you do also, and greater things than these shall you do.

One thing is certain, the claim of Jesus has never been disproved. It would be a weak argument to deny the possibility of something which we have not tried. As a matter of fact, those who have even partially imbibed the spirit of Christ have found comfort and a sense of well-being. It is indeed a good thing for us to re-evaluate and re-emphasize the whole teaching of this master mind, individually and collectively. Since other methods have failed, we should follow his instruction, daring to leave the results with God.

Like Plato and many others, but more clearly, he believed that the pattern of everything on earth is in heaven, meaning "at the center of things." The things on earth are copies of the things in heaven. When we work our way back to the pattern the copy will become transformed, as one of his followers said, "by the renewing of our minds." The consciousness of Jesus functioned in the realm of these patterns but also extended from the pattern to the copy, therefore, when he lifted the weight of condemnation from the copy he also removed the burden of that condemnation. The pattern was revealed and the lame walked.

Somewhere along the line we must add to our sincere belief in the philosophy of the Great Revelator an equal conviction that he used a power which responded to him as a natural law. It will be a new departure in human experience when increasing numbers of persons following the Master find not alone hope and comfort but learn how to use their spiritual power for definite purposes.

How do we know but that even what we call natural catastrophies, termed "acts of God," are themselves the result of mass confusion? This may not appeal to what we fondly call common sense. However, if the best common sense has done is to throw humanity into such confusion that the entire race trembles with the apprehension of what is to come, it might be worth while to find some deeper meaning to life which could keep us from a final step into complete chaos, and possibly the utter destruction of civilization as we now understand it.

If there is anything necessary to the salvation of humanity it is that an ever increasing number of individuals shall seek out the spiritual center within and learn to live from a consciousness of their unity with God. Since this has never been tried, it is worth the experiment. Anyone who follows this path will be following the leading of the Spirit within him. In so doing he will discover God for himself, and in this way help to bring the Kingdom of God to earth.

We are so likely to think that spiritual things are not for everyday living; that while the Kingdom of Heaven is something to believe in it is not something that is at hand; that while God is real to us in the sense that we believe in Him, spiritual power in action is something beyond our present life. Not so with Jesus. Jubilantly he proclaimed the Kingdom is at hand. He said this Kingdom is transcendent, not merely in the sense that we find consolation through hope, but also consummation in act.

On one occasion Jesus took Peter, James and John up into a high mountain where he became transfigured before them. The Kingdom of God is always on the mountain top of awareness. The Master took the three disciples whose spiritual awareness was ready for the vision. This vision is not withheld from the rest of us, rather, we withhold ourselves from it.

The Kingdom of God is at hand, waiting to be perceived. It is as though we were traveling through a country and suddenly came upon unexpected beauty. The beauty was always there but, like Plato's cavemen, we are blindfolded. "Eyes have they, but they see not; ears have they, but they hear not." It is through communion with the Spirit that the human is elevated to the Divine, that limitation passes from bondage into freedom, and earth becomes "crammed full of God." Surely, Christ is with us and we may behold his face, dare we look upon it.

When the disciples saw the face of Jesus illumined with celestial light they fell upon the earth and were sore afraid. He touched them, saying, "arise, and be not afraid." He told them this heavenly light is natural, even here on earth, because God's Kingdom is here and now. The Christ which Peter recognized in Jesus is present, waiting our recognition. Nothing stands between this heavenly Christ and the earthly man but our unbelief. Should we not take hope? Should we not go, as the Illumined One did, into the mountain top of the Spirit where Christ awaits us?

This divine union, dimly perceived in all religions, shone full-orbed in the life of Jesus who gloriously trod this planet with one hand in the hand of God and the other in the hand of humanity. This divine meeting in our individual lives is not "some far-off divine event toward which the whole creation moves," but rather, a divine reality in which the whole drama of creation and human experience takes place. The Man of God saw beyond the bard's vision, not to something which is to become, but to that which is.

"And when they had lifted up their eyes, they saw no man, save Jesus only." It is when we look up that we behold the face of no man save him only who is the son of God. Jesus gives us back to ourselves, thus restoring (or finding) the lost sheep of Israel. The Good Shepherd brings all into the divine fold. The Good Shepherd is the gate, the way, the truth and the life.

This Good Shepherd is God in us; the eternal Father forever begetting his beloved son in us. It is this eternal begetting of the Spirit in our consciousness that transforms the old man, transmuting the lower nature into its divine and spiritual pattern. This transmutation takes place in the mountain top of intuitive revelation as we look up and behold the face of Him only.

Turning to his disciples, the Master asked, "Whom do men say I, the son of man, am?" They answered that some said he was John the Baptist, some Elias, and others that he was one of the prophets. This did not satisfy Jesus. He knew that everyone is an individual manifestation of God and that he could not possibly be someone else. Everyone must be himself. Everyone must be in a unique relationship to the whole. Turning again to them he asked, "But whom say ye that I am?" He wanted to find out if his disciples really understood what he was trying to tell them.

Peter answered, saying, "Thou art the Christ, the

Son of the living God." For this answer Jesus blessed Peter, saying, ". . . for flesh and blood hath not revealed it unto thee, but my Father which is in heaven." And he added, "Thou art Peter . . . Upon this rock I will build my church, and the gates of hell shall not prevail against it."

Peter stands for spiritual awareness; the church, for that temple not made with hands, eternal in the heavens, and the gates of hell for the suppositional opposite to good, summed up in the term evil or that which denies the Spirit. It was not Peter, the man, to whom Jesus referred as a rock (the rock of salvation, or the rock in a weary land where people found shelter from the burning sun). It was the inward awareness of Peter that he referred to as the rock (the shelter in a time of storm).

He told his followers he had come to save that which was lost. He said that it is the will of God that not one of these little ones should perish. It is self-evident that God, who is life, cannot will death; that the Divine Spirit, which is joy, cannot will sadness. God can will only good, give only life, and be only love. Jesus said he had come to restore that which was lost. He did not say he had come to create something new or to do something that God had failed to accomplish. He said he had come to restore. Nothing can be restored unless it first exists. Always we find this enlightened soul was speaking of a spiritual man and a spiritual kingdom, which, though obscure, is always here.

The Wayshower came to lead us out of fear and doubt into a pathway of certainty. Gently, firmly, sometimes almost vehemently, he proclaimed the way, the truth and the life. We should not let him stand apart from us. We should open our vision that his may become ours, that together we may explore that heavenly country which is the natural habitat of the soul.

And now we come to one of the promises that is filled with great meaning: "If two of you shall agree on earth, as touching anything that they shall ask, it shall be done for them of my Father which is in heaven. For where two or three are gathered together in my name, there am I in the midst of them." If Jesus really knew what he was talking about, the thought of groups of people could actually use such a spiritual power that the very gates of heaven would be opened and a divine outpouring come to all.

It is a lack of the ability to get together that brings trouble to the world. Out of a lack of common purpose and effort, and the confusion which follows, comes a universal sense of insecurity, making men and nations alike distrustful of each other. Until there is a collective faith in God the world will remain in confusion.

We cannot instantly convert the thought of the world. We are brought back to the only thing we can convert, our individual consciousness, hoping and believing that in so doing we shall prove the teaching of Jesus. This is the first step in the uniting of our spiritual forces for the common good that the Fatherhood of God may manifest not only in individual sonship but equally in the brotherhood of man.

It has been said that "religions are many, but Religion is one." The varying beliefs of mankind are unnumbered, but the primal faith of the race is today, as of old, the One Faith, an instinctive reliance upon the Unseen. Religion is one. Faith is one. Truth is one. Old forms, old creeds are passing, but the eternal realities abide. Religion has not been destroyed, it is being discovered. God, the great innovator, is in His world and progress is by divine authority.

It is the duty, the privilege, and it should be the joy, of those who have faith to unite their conviction, thus creating a great field of faith. This multiplication of conviction is more than adding one individual effort to another. Weaving them together makes them like a strong rope, the individual strands of which can sustain only a fraction of the weight that the close weaving together can lift.

Here is an experiment as yet untried. While it is true that individual groups do unite themselves for definite purposes, as a social set, a political party, a commercial enterprise, or a national spirit, so far the very large numbers who have strong individual spiritual convictions have not united themselves in a common purpose for the salvation of humanity. We do not have many instances where even two or three persons of strong spiritual conviction have been willing to surrender their differences of opinion to one common spiritual purpose for the good of all. This alone can save the world.

No one yet knows what the united spiritual consciousness of a thousand persons could do. Before such a possibility could be demonstrated it would be necessary that those engaging in such an experiment agree on certain spiritual truths, surrendering all differences of opinion to one common purpose, and consciously use their faith for that purpose. They would not have to agree on every detail of belief, but they would have to unite in one purpose. They would have to pray and meditate without ceasing for that purpose even though they were otherwise engaged in the ordinary activities of life.

Since this experiment has never been tried no one can deny its possibility. If Jesus knew what he was talking about, such an experiment would be successful. Suppose it were tried in times of impending trouble, in times of national and international crisis. It was the simple and direct statement of the Wayshower that such a collective consciousness can produce magnificent results.

We cannot believe that the Kingdom of God is stormed by protest or coerced through the united effort of human beings. But we can believe that a spiritual force could be loosed through a conscious recognition of its action.

We already know that this is true in the individual life and we may assume that this individual power could be multiplied a million times through the joining together of even a thousand persons in one common purpose. Their effort would be deliberate and determined, their goal would be positively held in mind. Since most everything else has failed, and the hope of the world today hangs in a balance, no greater good could come to humanity than that such a group of people band themselves together with the express purpose of demonstrating spiritual power in human affairs.

An illustration of this was given following the crucifixion of Jesus. After his resurrection he was seen of his followers for at least forty days, "to whom also he showed himself alive after his passion by many infallible proofs, being seen of them forty days and speaking of the things pertaining to the kingdom of God . . . And when the day of Pentecost was fully come, they were all with one accord in one place." And suddenly they were filled with the Holy Ghost.

It was through collective prayer and collective listening that this small but fervent group—among whom were many who had known the Master personally—received the benediction of the Spirit. Remaining in continual prayer, a field of faith and conviction was formed, permitting one of the most amazing experiences in all human history to transpire. This should show us the advisability of creating a group consciousness where each adds his faith to the collective expectancy. This makes possible a more complete manifestation of spiritual power. It was the loosing of this spiritual power through the fervor of faith which is spoken of in the second chapter of Acts as the day of Pentecost when all were filled with the Holy Ghost.

No man ever lived who valued the individual life more than Jesus. He proclaimed his divinity through his humanity, and taught that all men are brothers. As the divinity of Christ is awakened through the humanity of man, the divine spark shot from the central fires of the Universal Flame warms other souls in the glow of its own self-realization.

Like Jesus, Paul was an individualist, and like the Master, he saw variety in unity, the individualization of the One in the many, the passing of the creative Spirit into the breath of every man's life. "Now there are diversities of gifts, but the same Spirit . . . it is the same God which worketh all in all . . . the self-same Spirit, dividing to every man . . . by one Spirit we are all baptized into one body, whether we be Jews or Gentiles, whether we be bond or free . . . ye are the body of Christ, and members in particular."

This was the teaching of Jesus and Paul. Indeed, it is the great teaching of the scriptures of the ages and is not to be lightly treated or carelessly dealt with. This idea of the unity of all life means exactly what it says, and not something else.

What would happen if we came to understand that our individual mentalities are the Universal Mind in us, that the law of our individual lives is the one Universal Law used in individual ways? If this is true we cannot hope to find deliverance from bondage until we first subject our thought, will and purpose to the supreme Intelligence, divine Love and perfect Law which is the final reality of our being.

Jesus made this complete surrender. We do not know what would happen in our lives should we make it, other than by the study of his life. Why is it that we do not make this surrender? The first reason is that we do not actually believe. We have sort of spiritualized away the teaching of Jesus as though it referred to a life impossible to be lived on this earth. Another and perhaps the most important reason is that we are afraid we might lose our individual being in the great ocean of life. Self-preservation is the first law of nature, psychologically and spiritually as well as physically.

Our conflicts will be resolved when we realize the surrender is not to the loss of individuality but to the discovery of it. The expression, "Hid with Christ in God," does not mean submerged or lost in Christ. It means immersion; the discovery of the self in God; the finding of that something within us, the echo of whose reality is present both in the soul and in the intellect. Jesus and his followers were not on a pathway of self-annihilation. Their philosophy was not one of nihilism. It was a philosophy of the unity of all life.

We humans desire love, appreciation and understanding above everything else. But who has made a complete surrender of himself to that love which gives all, asking nothing in return? The very nature of our being demands this kind of surrender. We all wish more life and the Blessed One tells us that he came that we might have life, and have it more abundantly. Have we surrendered everything that denies this life, even to the fear of death itself?

Jesus said he came to bring joy. Have we surrendered our unhappiness into the hands of joy? Or have we tried to make the surrender as though joy would give itself to us while we denied it to others? Jesus said, I bring a peace unto you which is not of this world—"My peace I give unto you." Have we surrendered confusion into the hands of peace so that we are no longer troubled in spirit? Jesus said, I bring you divine forgivingness, so complete that even all your mistakes shall be wiped out. Have we surrendered our human unforgivingness into the love of this all-comprehensive forgivingness?

The Great Revelator laid down the rules for the game of life. He had found the keys to the Kingdom of Heaven. He had unlocked the door and entered. He had found the light. Have we surrendered our darkness into this light?

He proclaimed the more abundant life. He said, in effect: "Let your good be a symbol of the greater good. Do not hold your good where thieves break in and steal or moths corrupt. Distribute it to the four winds of heaven and lo, it will return to you multiplied." It is only when we permit one side of our being to merge with the Infinite that we find the other side releasing divine energies and potentials which are possible alone to God. Entering the stream of life we are carried along on an infinite ocean of possibility.

Is it so difficult, then, to make this surrender? The answer must be both "Yes" and "No"—yes, because it is simple; no, because in the process we are stripped bare until pride and conceit are winnowed in the breezes of heaven, until nothing is left but the divine ideal which alone can invigorate our whole being. Who loses all shall gain all.

". . . and no man knoweth the Son, but the Father; neither knoweth any man the Father, save the Son." There is a place within each which knows the Father and is known of the Father; there is a place in the son which reveals the Father. When the Father is revealed the son likewise becomes known, because the Father and the son are one in essence. When the son turns to the Father, blending his nature with the Divine and receiving back from the Spirit that revelation which comes through intimate and conscious communion, the son truly reveals the Father.

Jesus assumed that there should be such an intimate relationship between the Universal and the individual, between the Father and the son. He said that when this relationship is rightly understood the labor of life will be transformed into a joy in living. "Come unto me, all ye that labour and are heavy laden, and I will give you rest." He knew that the ages could not come to him as a physical personality. He was speaking of the universal Christ, the Sonship within each, and its relationship to the Father who never forsakes the son.

In so far as it is possible for a human to take the place of God before men, Jesus did so, becoming a revelator of the Divine Nature and the complete unity of all life. In so far as it is humanly possible his words actually were the words of God. Through them the Divine was revealed by one who had completely entered into union with life.

The search after God is not God. The search is a way, an endeavor to find God. But when one finds God he finds himself not submerged in but saturated with life. Nirvana is not absorption but immersion.

We cannot expect this complete union until we first surrender everything contrary to the nature of goodness, truth, beauty and wisdom. But when we do this the Spirit flows through our thought and act. Its power is delivered through our faith and belief, and life finds a fresh starting point in us for the manifestation of its creative urge. If we believe in the teaching of the Master we must expect to find the fountain of life at the center of our own being and the miracle of love in our own act.

The difference between Jesus and most of us was that his idea of coming to God for the easing of burdens was not morbid. With joy he saw the final outcome, the complete salvation, the ultimate triumph of the Spirit. "For my yoke is easy, and my burden is light." Jesus was free from fear. Joy had entered his soul. Peace had passed into his being. Gladness flowed through him, sometimes quietly and sometimes almost turbulently, with the joy of living.

It would be a mistake to overlook the joy of his teaching. We are not only to come in quietness and in peace to the divine center of our being, we should come in joy and with gladness. It is not a funeral dirge but a hymn of praise we should sing. The spiritual yoke is easy and its burden light.

It was difficult for the contemporaries of Jesus to follow his divine logic to the revelation of the Son of God within themselves. Their philosophy was materialistic, a philosophy of separatism which finally leads to nihilism. His philosophy, starting with the most external fact in nature, led him back to the interior meaning of all facts and to the discovery of the ultimate cause concealed in every effect.

When they questioned his authority and asked, ". . . who makest thou thyself?" saying that they had Abraham to their father, Jesus' reply was, "Verily I say unto you, Before Abraham was, I am." This completely confused them and they viewed him as one who was distraught of mind. He answered them by saying that "Abraham rejoiced to see my day, and he saw it and was glad."

One of our difficulties in perceiving the changeless truth that the Great Teacher said could make us free is that we live in a world of continual change. Because everything changes rapidly around us it is difficult to vision a changeless reality. This intellectual difficulty is met when we realize that change takes place within the changeless. The ceaseless movement of life is but a necessary complement of that which does not move. It is life viewing itself in action that it may come into self-realization through fruition. There is a center in everyone that never moves.

Perhaps it will be easier to understand this if we view our lives in retrospect, thinking back through the ceaseless surge and flow of change that has taken place in our experience. It is evident that something has strung all these experiences on one beginningless and endless thread of continuity. This thread has bound all these experiences together. We pass from one experience to another without in any way affecting the Life Principle Itself. But because our imagination and emotion are so often caught in experience, we are likely to think that it is the experience that is using us rather than our using it.

Jesus tells us to reverse this process of thought and realize that there is a center of continuity, something which existed before Abraham was, and something which will continue when this physical form disintegrates. This is Life Itself, the son proceeding from the Father, the individual immersed in the Universal. It is this impartation of universal life through the individual that gives us the ability to live and the power to act.

The Master tells us to follow the thread of our lives back to the original loom. He is not telling us to disconnect this thread, nor that it is to become absorbed or lost. Quite the reverse. He tells us that who loses his life shall find it—who loses his isolation shall find himself one in an infinite inclusion. He will discover himself not only one with and in God, but a unique and individual presentation of God. Jesus was the greatest individualist who ever lived, yet, at the same time, he was the greatest inclusionist because he included the individual in the Universal.

This is the true meaning of Sonship, that each has the whole at his disposal. Therefore, there can be no limit to the expansion of the individual. We are always expanding into the infinite, but never becoming the infinite. If we could become the infinite we would be absorbed in the infinite. This was not the teaching of Jesus. He believed in eternal expansion with no point of saturation.

CHAPTER XI

Divine Sonship

When Jesus asked the Pharisees, "What think ye of Christ? Whose son is he?" they answered that Christ is the son of David. It was to the insight of Peter that the real meaning of Christ was revealed, for he said of Jesus, "Thou art the Christ, son of the living God." It remained for Jesus to make the explanation complete.

Christ, the Son, and God, the Father, are one in essence. The life of God is the life in man. The universal Spirit is also the spirit of the individual man and the Father of all creation. There is, as Emerson said, "one mind common to all individual men." "He who is the son is one with Him who is the Father." The difference is not in essence, but in degree.

The Father is always greater than the son. But everyone can say, "My life is God," or "God is my life." Not all of God, of course, since no one can encompass the infinite. We are of like nature to the universal Spirit, one with It, of It and in It. Its essence and intelligence flow through us, making us what we are. Thus Jesus said of the son, as though God were talking to him, ". . . sit thou on my right hand and I will make thine enemies thy footstool."

To sit on the "right hand" means a right relationship with the Father. When this relationship is established by the son all that does not belong to the heavenly Kingdom is placed under foot. Everything that stands for limitation, fear, uncertainty and wrong becomes a footstool. It is this relationship with the infinite that we all must establish—a divine partnership in which the senior Partner is nothing less than the limitless love, the divine beneficence and the omnipotent power of the Spirit Itself.

Should we not, then, enter into this divine alliance with joy and thanksgiving? Would it be too much to say that the Divine Spirit must see and know us only as It knows Itself in us, must act for us only as It acts through us, must think and will in us only as our thinking and willing become subject to Its truth, Its beauty, Its love, and Its perfection?

"And whosoever shall exalt himself shall be abased, and he that humbleth himself shall be exalted." Not that God is pleased because we humble ourselves before Him, but when our ego gets in the way it blocks the divine light. "Ye make clean the outside of the cup, and of the platter, but within they are full of extortion and excess. Cleanse first that which is within the cup, and the platter, and the outside will be clean also." The issues of life are from within. If a man is pure in heart, what he does will be pure in act. If he is kind in his thought, what he does will be kind. It is the inside of the cup that needs cleansing.

It is the childlike mind that meets the Divine face to face. There need be no formality in our coming to God. The approach is simple and direct, a spontaneous act of faith and trust. Through long years of patient endeavor Jesus had learned this simple truth. This is why he taught no methods of severity, no intellectual formulas for the spiritualization of thought, no medium or mediator between the intellect and the Father other than the divinity within which stands at the doorway of consciousness waiting for the intellect to become aware of its presence.

Perhaps the best known of the parables of Jesus is the story of the prodigal son. It is the story of each one of us, for we all have left our father's house and wandered into a far country. He begins this famous parable by telling the story of a father who had two sons. It seems that the younger of the sons came to his father and asked for his portion of the family estate for he wanted to be completely independent of his father. The father did not argue with the son or ask him what he was going to do, but divided his portion to him.

The young man, who now felt quite free to do as he pleased, took the money his father gave him and went into a far country. This "far country" represents a state of separation from the source of life. We travel into this far country when we separate ourselves from Spirit and try to go entirely on our own, as though we were isolated beings.

The young man soon wasted his substance in riotous living, but when he had spent everything "a great famine arose in that land" and he found himself in want. A famine always arises when we separate ourselves from daily communion with the Spirit. It is then that we begin to be in want. The waters of our individual lives soon dry up when we separate ourselves from the well-spring of being.

Having exhausted his resources the prodigal was compelled to sell his services to a citizen of the far country into which he had traveled and soon he was sent into the field to feed swine. Perhaps the Master used this comparison to show what a complete state of destitution the once well-cared-for young man had fallen into. Jesus was talking to those who held the meat of swine to be unholy. Therefore, he was placing the plight of the young man in the worst possible light. He had fallen to such low estate that he was a complete social outcast.

But the Great Teacher paints an even more dreary picture, for he said that the young man became so famished that he would gladly have eaten the husks that the swine were fed. "But no man gave unto him." This is similar to the story of the foolish virgins to whom no one gave oil, for God had already filled their vessels to overflowing but they had refused to let the divine light burn on the altar of a consecrated union. Others may give us temporary food, clothing and shelter, but life alone can give life. This is the meaning of the words, "No man gave unto him."

And now a remarkable thing happened to the young man. "He came to himself." This is one of the most important parts of the story. No matter how isolated from the source of life we seem to be, there is always something within us that can come to itself.

How could this be unless there were a Real Self to which we may awaken? There is some part of our being that never descends to the lower levels of chaotic experience. Always there is a Presence with us and we can never entirely escape Its beneficent influence. Always there is a pool of Spirit into which we may plunge. But first we must remember who we are, we must find our divine center.

And when he "came to himself" the young man remembered that in his father's house there had always been bread to eat. There had been servants. There had been luxury. There had been the fruit of the vine and the warmth of home. Remembering, hope sprang up within him and he resolved to return to his father's house.

But, as with all of us, he had a deep sense of guilt because of what he had done. He said to himself that when he met his father he would throw himself in the dust before him, confess his shame and ask to be forgiven, without hoping actually to be reinstated. Of course, he could not really be reinstated. He would ask that he become as a servant in the house. At least this would give him protection, food and shelter. He would be humble and meek because he knew himself to be so unworthy.

Everyone makes this confession to himself. Everyone resolves to return to the father's house. And though we may feel unworthy, there is always an inward sense that somehow everything can be made right if we can only get back to the father. There is a voice within that has never ceased speaking to us, a presence that has never ceased beckoning to us, a power greater than we which has willed that we make this return journey.

And so the young man started on his homeward journey filled with both hope and despair, walking down the lonely road with tearful and downcast eyes, yet with a conviction stronger than his fears. Unless our faith were greater than our fears none of us could make this return journey. Life has willed it so, and unknowingly the young man was following an intuition implanted from the foundation of creation—the knowledge that all shall finally come to a place of peace in conscious union with the Divine.

While the young man was yet afar off the father saw him and ran out to meet him and kissed him. This is one of the most glorious parts of the whole story because it teaches us that God turns to us as we turn to Him. We have but to make the choice and the Divine Presence draws close to us, embracing us in Its perfect love and wisdom. It is a repetition of that other thought of Jesus where he said that everyone who knocks will gain entrance, everyone who seeks will find, everyone who asks will receive. How could this be unless the gift of life had already been made from the foundation of the world? How could this be unless life had willed it so? It could not.

The young man threw himself down before his father, saying that he was no more worthy to be called a son. This confession was good for him, as it is good for all of us. It is a purging of the soul and the mind by some inward fire which burns out the accumulated experiences of all the misspent time of folly.

Again Jesus tells us of our true relationship with God. He tells us that the father did not argue with the son. He did not condemn him. He did not ask where he had been or what he had been doing. He

did not say, "You are unworthy to be my son."
Rather, he told the servants to bring the best robe
for him, a ring for his hand and shoes for his feet.
He told them to prepare a feast that they might rejoice because his son who was dead was alive again,
because that which was lost had been found.

Divine givingness always implies an equal divine
forgivingness. That which gives all asks only that we
return the gift to the Giver. And behold, when this
is done, the feast is already spread, the divine banquet
has begun.

The young man, in ignorance, had departed from
his father's house. Under divine guidance he had returned. The father was there, the house was there,
the servants were there, the law of good was ready to
serve him. The table was spread, the banquet was
prepared, and the feast which had been interrupted
by his departure continued.

And now we come to another part of this remarkable story. It is about the elder son who was working
in the fields when his young brother returned. Hear-
ing music he called one of the servants and asked what
was the occasion for such merry-making. When he
was told that his brother had returned and a feast had
been prepared for him, he became angry and would
not go in to the feast.

This elder son had an attitude of self-righteous bigotry that we all recognize in ourselves. He had been

living in his father's house all the time, but he was living there from a sense of stern duty. The spontaneous joy of living had never flooded his life with warmth and color. He was good in a negative way. Jesus demands that we be good in a positive way. He said that he had come that we might have more abundant life, that his peace and joy might enter into us and that the certainty of the love of God might bring to each the divine assurance of peace and security.

Just as the father did not argue with the younger son when he went into the far country, so he did not argue with the elder son who remained at home. When the elder son complained the father said to him, "Son, thou art ever with me, and all that I have is thine." It is as though the father said to him, "My dear boy, why didn't you make merry with your friends? Why haven't you enjoyed the home in which you have been living? Surely," he says to the elder son, "you would not cast out your younger brother who has returned to his home. Come in and make merry with us. Forgive and forget." This was not a rebuke to the elder son, it was an explanation of his true relationship with the father.

Each of us is a combination of these two sons. We refuse to enter into the father's house and we will not allow others to enter. But our sin is more largely of ignorance than of intent. Just as the younger son did not know that he must soon spend his substance, since all he could carry with him would be so limited, so the elder son did not realize that he had substance to spend. One traveled into a far country to discover his error; the other remained at home and failed to discover his mistake.

"And I, if I be lifted up from the earth, will draw all men unto me . . . As Moses lifted up the serpent in the wilderness, even so must the son of man be lifted up." In antiquity "serpent" stood for the Life Principle. Thus we find it was a serpent that tempted Eve, which means a wrong use of the Life Principle. It was the same serpent or Life Principle that Moses lifted up in the wilderness, upon which the children of Israel looked and were healed. It is this lifting up of the Life Principle that is necessary. Life must be accepted either as good or evil.

As Moses had lifted up the serpent, or elevated the Life Principle to spiritual awareness, so Jesus repeated the process on a higher level by lifting up the idea of sonship, a sonship which is created in heaven and maintained on earth but which is not of this earth but from heaven. Therefore, the son of man must be lifted up from the earth, that is, we must come to know that our nature is spiritual. Lifting up the idea of this inward divinity is lifting up the son of man from the earth. The physical man is of this earth, the spiritual man is from heaven. It is when we lift our earthly image up to its heavenly likeness that we discover the true nature of man.

It was the mission of Jesus to reveal the spiritual to the physical, to lift up the physical to the spiritual. "I am come a light into the world, that whosoever believeth on me shall not abide in darkness." He often referred to that light which is not seen on land or sea, the inner light that lights every man's pathway, the light in which there is no darkness, the light which is eternal. Those who enter into this light no longer live in darkness.

If we knew, with complete certainty, that the light is always there we would most certainly turn toward it. This is what Jesus told us. This was his ministry. The light is always there. Our darkness is merely a shadow marking the place where we obstruct the light.

Paul tells us continually to give thanks unto the Father through whose love we become "partakers of the inheritance of the saints in light" and "who . . . hath delivered us from the power of darkness and hath translated us into the kingdom of his dear Son." The struggle of humanity is to discover that light which lights every man's path. The Apostle emphasizes the need of continual prayer and meditation, turning our thoughts toward the good, living in conscious communion with God, the Father, and with that spiritual essence which is hid in every form. In this way we come into the light of the Spirit.

Paul had a deep and worshipful reverence for Jesus, the man. He had an equally deep understanding of Christ, the Universal Son, incarnated in everyone. It is this Universal Sonship that he refers to when he says that God has "translated us into the kingdom of his dear Son." "Translated" does not mean to be transformed or to become transformed. Rather, it means to understand the true status of something that already exists.

The redemption which causes us to become partakers of the inheritance is a redemption of light over darkness. Paul speaks of this redemption as being through the blood of the beloved Son under the forgiveness of our sins. According to the authorities, the blood which cleanses is "the divine truth proceeding from the Lord. It is life outpoured." It is the cleansing fluid from Emmanuel's veins—Emmanuel meaning God-with-us.

Christ is the perfect and divine man. Through our spiritual nature we may become aware of Christ within us, "who is the image of the invisible God, the firstborn of every creature." The first born of every creature is the pattern, the spiritual prototype of all creation. It is the word of God which becomes flesh and dwells among us, not only in the person of Jesus but as the principle of all created form.

". . . it pleased the Father that in him should all fulness dwell." All fullness means the essence of Spirit, which, flowing through creation, becomes the potential power of that which is created. It is the passing of Spirit into form through Its own self-contemplation. It is the word become flesh. It is the Law of God manifesting Itself in the physical universe. "The blood of the lamb" is the continual flow of spiritual life animating everything, while "the lamb slain from the foundations of the world" is a symbol of the outpouring of Spirit.

Paul's description of Christ is a description of the Universal Son which he refers to as the great mystery "even the mystery which hath been hid from ages . . . which is Christ in you the hope of glory." It was to this Universal Sonship that Jesus referred when he said, "Before Abraham was, I am." Paul tells us that we are complete in him and that "buried with him in baptism" we rise with him in faith. To be buried in baptism means to become conscious that we are immersed in the living waters of life. From this consciousness the whole man, through faith, rises with Christ into the liberty of the sons of God.

Those who are "risen with Christ seek those things which are above." Their inward vision turns to the spiritual prototypes, the divine patterns of life. They set their "affection on things above, not on things on the earth." Hence the Apostle tells us, "When

Christ, who is our life, shall appear, then shall ye also appear with him in glory." It is the birth of this eternal Son in us that is spoken of as the "new birth."

When this new birth takes place "there is neither Greek nor Jew, circumcision nor uncircumcision . . . bond or free, but Christ is all and in all." When each reaches the summit of his own ascent he will discover innumerable other summits, each watered by the same Divine Spirit, each standing in the same light. Christ, or the Divine Son, will then be all-in-all, whether Jew or Greek, whether barbarian or bond or free.

As Paul continues his instruction he says, "Let the peace of God rule in your hearts" and "the word of Christ dwell in you richly in all wisdom" and "whatsoever ye do, do it heartily as unto the Lord . . . But he that doeth wrong shall receive for the wrong which he hath done: and there is no respect of persons." This is the old teaching of an eye for an eye and a tooth for a tooth, the inevitable operation of the law of cause and effect. This is not a harsh but a careful analysis, one to which common sense can subscribe sanity and with which both reason and revelation can agree.

Paul tells us it is high time for us to awake from our deep sleep of ignorance, fear and superstition, to the glorious liberty of the sons of light. We must awake to the fact that we are immersed in the living Spirit, in the waters of life.

The Apostle John expressed it this way: "Beloved, now are we the sons of God." There is no future in the Spirit. The nature of reality cannot change. If we are ever to become sons of God it will be because we already are sons of God. "Beloved, now are we the sons of God, and it doth not yet appear what we shall be." Here John implies that what has been given is not yet perceived, even though the gift has been made. There is a depth to our spiritual nature which eternity alone can reveal. Evolution does not create this divine nature but is a progressive awakening to it. "It doth not yet appear what we shall be, but we know that when he shall appear, we shall be like him, for we shall see him as he is."

This is one of the most significant passages in the outstanding philosophy of the ages. It implies that there is something to which we must awake. It is already awake to us. Our quest is to the discovery of something that already exists. It is inevitable that freedom shall finally come to everyone. The truth is already known in Spirit and becomes known to us through a close and conscious communion with the Divine Presence. "And every man that hath this hope in him purifieth himself even as he is pure." This "he" is Christ in us.

Jesus had said that every man's prayer is answered according to his conviction. "Verily I say unto you, they have their reward." Paul reiterated, " . . . and every man shall receive his own reward according to his own labour." The hidden laws of cause and effect are used mostly in ignorance but they are never violated. Every man lives unto himself. Every man lives alone in God while at the same time we all live unto every other person in God because the Spirit is in everyone.

Surely no one would seek to harm another if he knew that in so doing he must bring hurt to himself. And none would seek to lose his identity in others if he knew that every man has a unique identity in God. There is an integrity to the soul. Therefore Paul said, " . . . let no man glory in men, for all things are yours . . . or the world, or life, or death, or things present, or things to come; all are yours and ye are Christ's and Christ's is God's." This is a statement of absolute and inseparable unity binding the past, the present and the future into one sequence, tying the life of the individual back to Christ, the generic or universal Son, and to God, who manifests Himself through the son.

Both Jesus and Paul have been misunderstood by the ages. Yet, Christian theology announces the unity of the Trinity. We all are individual members of One Sonship through which God, the Universal

Father, is forever giving birth to His Son. When we realize that God, the Father, is forever giving new birth to us, then we shall discover a springing up to newness of life within which is perennial in its spring-time, everlasting in its blossoming, and eternal in its fruitage—the Garden of Eden in the soul of man.

"For though ye have ten thousand instructors in Christ, yet have ye not many fathers . . . But he that is joined unto the Lord is one spirit," said Paul. The Spirit of the One runs through the all. Therefore, he that is joined unto the Lord is one Spirit.

Throughout the teaching of Jesus and Paul we find this central theme. If the two greatest characters in the New Testament laid such emphasis on the unity of the Spirit, we, who seek to discover the hidden meaning of their teaching, should ponder long and earnestly over the implications of these utterances that lead us back to the unity of all life. As there is One Spirit, One Father, so there can be but One Son.

The whole search of humanity is after this unity. By some divine intuition implanted within the soul we know that there is a life beyond this life, that there is a livingness within this life, the possibilities of which we but dimly perceive. We should take time for meditation, contemplation and prayer, en-deavoring to reach back to the origin of our source in the fountain of all life.

While we have one common source, Divine Wisdom has seen fit to make each an individual. Unity does not mean uniformity. There is unity at the center, with infinite variation at the circumference. Hence Paul said, " . . . as the Lord hath called every one, so let him walk. And so ordain I in all churches . . . Circumcision is nothing, and uncircumcision is nothing . . . Let every man abide in the same calling wherein he was called . . . let every man, wherein he is called, therein abide with God."

The reins of our individuality should run full length. We should not be so concerned with the outward forms as with the fact that they are all bound back to a unified center. Variety in unity is the keynote of true spiritual philosophy. We find these variations in all nature. We find them in all humanity. And we must expect to find them in the individual members of the body of Christ, "which members we are." But at the center is the supreme Spirit Itself giving rise to all individual forms, which individual forms are watered and fed from one source.

On the eve of his departure from this world, having sent Judas on his mission of betrayal, Jesus turned to his small group and told them to love one another even as he had loved them. He told them not to be afraid, that all people are immortal and that in time they would rejoin him. The spiritual sun is forever rising, but it can never set. Life will always be more, never less. Our life is a pathway of an eternal expansion. Therefore, Jesus said, "Do not be troubled in heart," and to his immediate disciples, "I go and prepare a place for you . . . that where I am ye may be also."

Thomas said to Jesus, "We know not whither thou goest, and how can we know the way? Jesus saith unto him, I am the way, the truth, and the life: no man cometh unto the Father, but by me." It is impossible to come to the Universal Spirit other than through the doorway of spiritual awareness. We come unto the Father through the Son incarnated in us. Therefore, the Christed One said, "I am the way, the truth, and the life." Our spiritual nature, Christ within us, is "the way, the truth, and the life." It is through the Son in us that the Father is revealed to us.

Philip could not comprehend this and said, "Lord, show us the Father, and it sufficeth us." And Jesus said to Philip, "He that hath seen me hath seen the Father . . . the Father that dwelleth in me, he doeth the works." Realizing that they did not understand the full significance of this great revelation, he said, if you cannot believe me because of what I say, or understand what I mean, "believe me for the very work's sake."

The signs or works that followed the words of Jesus were results of his communion with the Spirit and his use of spiritual law. He made no claim for himself that he did not make for all. He said, in essence, "Whether or not you fully comprehend the meaning of my words you can at least see the results of my spiritual communion." "He that believeth on me, the works that I do shall he do also."

To make this teaching even more explicit he said, "If ye ask anything in my name, I will do it." Moses had said that the name of God is "I am"; that the word of power is in our own mouth. Jesus said that he came not to destroy but to fulfill. "I am" is a statement of the verb "to be" and since it is impossible to speak or think without using some part of the verb "to be," this word is always in our mouths. Our consciousness is enveloped in it. We are always using the law of life whether we know it or not.

Moses had already taught this from the standpoint of an immutable law of cause and effect—an eye for an eye, a tooth for a tooth. He had told his followers about the universal "I am." He had taught that God is one. He had taught the great law of cause and effect which governs everything.

What Jesus added to this was the relationship of the individual "I" to this universal "I am," the relationship of the Son to the Father, the necessity of using the laws of life from the high motivation of love. Therefore, he said that he would give them "the comforter that he may abide with you forever, even the spirit of truth whom the world cannot receive because it seeth him not, neither knoweth him, but ye know him, for he dwelleth with you and shall be in you."

Few statements of the Master are so fraught with meaning. The comforter, which is the spirit of truth, is in us and with us. It is the Spirit incarnated in everything and in all people. But this divine indwelling Presence must be consciously realized through our interior awareness. It is this interior awareness that has been spoken of as "the secret place of the most High." The comforter, then, which is to come, the spirit of truth which has all power, is already here and when we know it and see it the time of our not knowing and not seeing is as though it were not and never had been.

When Jesus gathered his few followers together at the Last Supper, washed their feet and told them to love one another and not to be afraid, he knew that he was about to leave them personally and physically. But they would not be alone because the "comforter" would come. He was preparing to lay down his human life and pass from their physical gaze, but was leaving in his place a realization of that Divine Presence which every man must discover for himself. He knew this to be the only salvation there is. He had shown them the way. They must follow it. "Yet a little while and the world seeth me no more, but ye see me."

And now comes a revelation of the great mystery of life: "I am in my Father, and ye in me, and I in you." The Christ, the Son of God, is always in the Father and we are always in the Christ and the Christ is always in us. The Father and the son are one, undivided and indivisible forever.

"Peace I leave with you. My peace I give unto you. Not as the world giveth, give I unto you. Let not your heart be troubled, neither let it be afraid." If there is anything we need it is peace of mind. Without it life is not worth while. Peace of mind comes only when there is a personal and collective sense of security. This sense of security comes when there is a sense of belonging to the universe. Jesus knew that no one is or ever can become sufficient unto himself. It is when the soul returns to its source and finds its true center in pure Spirit that it enters into that peace which the Wise One said the world cannot give.

He knew of a calm back of confusion. He knew of a love that consumes hate, of a unity that must dissolve separateness, a peace that passes human comprehension, because he knew God. He knew God as the very being of his own life, the heart of his heart, the soul of his soul. He knew God intimately. His sense of God was warm and colorful, almost dramatic.

He did not know God as a judge, for he knew that the law of cause and effect is the judge. He knew that there is justice without judgment. He did not know God as a tribal deity. He knew God as a Universal Presence centered in his own soul. Jesus knew God as Presence and Person.

There is a difference between a belief in God and a feeling that we are in the Divine Presence. It is this difference which is the dividing line between entering into the Spirit and viewing It as a thing apart. It is when we enter *into* the Spirit that we know God. No one can enter in for us. Each must make the great discovery for himself.

Somewhere along the line we shall all have to make this discovery and realize what the great Man of God meant when he said, "Hereafter I will not talk much with you. But the comforter, which is the Holy Ghost . . . shall teach you all things . . . These things have I spoken unto you that my joy might remain in you and that your joy might be full." He left but one admonition for the fulfillment of this peace and this joy: "This is my commandment, that ye love one another." God is love and we know God through love. Love is givingness and love is forgivingness; love is life and real life is revealed through love.

And now we come to another of those cosmic concepts in the teaching of the greatest spiritual genius of the ages: "Henceforth I call you not servants . . . but I have called you friends." This is not the relationship of master to slave but of equal with equal. The life of man is God and God's life is in man—not as two, separate and distinct, but as one, united and eternal.

It was this intimacy with the Spirit, this sense of belonging to It, that made Jesus the most exalted personality of the ages, towering spiritually above all others. It also made him the most human personality who ever lived. He had caught humanity up into Divinity without division and viewed the whole cosmos as one vast system of unity. Therefore he said, "Ye have not chosen me, but I have chosen you."

This is where the soul makes its great claim on God. This is where God makes His great demand on the soul. We did not create ourselves. Life is the high gift of heaven. Our human experience is but a process through which we awake to a Divinity imposed upon us, a Presence forever incarnated in us, a relationship with the universe which we did not even choose. The final realities of life rest not in man's desire but in God's will. The pearl of great price is not a jewel bought through human effort. There is nothing we have to offer in exchange for it. It is that which is given. This gift cannot be complete until it is received.

In his most passionate prayer for his disciples and

for all humanity Jesus prayed "that they all may be one; as thou, Father, art in me, and I in thee, that they also may be one in us." This prayer has reference to the deep and underlying unity of all life. "As thou, Father, art in me"—God is omnipresent, filling all space and every form. "As thou, Father, art in me, and I in thee"—the Father is in the son and the son is in the Father. God is all life. Nothing can be excluded from the One Presence, One Spirit and Power. "I in them, and thou in me, that they may be made perfect in one." Seeing ourselves in the One, knowing the One in all, awakens within us a consciousness of Divine Sonship and an inseparable union with the Universal Father.

"Sanctify them through thy truth: thy word is truth." It is difficult for us to grasp the full significance of his teaching about the word of truth. Yet, in all his instruction the Master makes plain that there is a word of power which flows from the consciousness that understands its true relationship with the Father.

It was his complete reliance on this word of truth that gave Jesus his power. We do not follow him into the complete grandeur of his high concept. Our mental and spiritual horizon is not pushed as far away as was his. Our mountains are lower and our valleys more narrow. But there is a spring in our mountains. There is a stream running through our valleys that can lead us back to the original source of life which was the well-spring of his inspiration.

It was his purpose to awaken in us the vision that he had, binding us back to the Father, thus making it possible for the Father to sanctify us through that word which is truth. Consequently, he said to Pilate, "To this end was I born, and for this cause came I into the world, that I should bear witness unto the truth . . . Everyone that is of the truth heareth my voice." Spiritual things are spiritually discerned.

Paul speaks of the life of Jesus as being "the revelation of the mystery which was kept secret since the world began." This mystery was revealed in some degree by Moses when he said that God is one and that we are the children of this One. The first part of the great mystery is the unity of all in the One and the activity of the One through all. The second part of the mystery, "hid from the foundations of the world," are the Divine Patterns of reality existing at the center of everything.

That which the Blessed One himself, and Paul, his most ardent follower, revealed through intuition and faith, Plato had proclaimed through logic and reason. The necessity of the universe being a spiritual system—one, undivided and indivisible unit in which are included all of its parts. The parts are not disunities but realities within a unity.

Paul beseeches the brethren "that they be perfectly joined together in the same mind." This mind is the mind of Christ. He said he had baptized them, not in his own name but with the baptism of the Spirit. The ritual of baptism is a symbol through which the one entering physical water pictures his conviction that he is immersed in the eternal waters of the living Spirit, the well-spring of life to which the Master referred when he said that he who drinks from it shall never thirst again.

The Apostle assures us that without inward realization the cross of Christ itself has no meaning. The cross means the tree of life, the lower part of which is rooted in this world while the upper part reaches to heaven. The cross beam represents the sheltering influence as the light from heaven casts its shadow of protection on earth. Paul said that the mystery of the cross will "destroy the wisdom of the wise and bring to nothing the understanding of the prudent." The intellect alone cannot understand the mystery of the Kingdom of God. It can merely lead our reasoning faculty to a place where it must stand aside and permit the divine event to take place, the flowing of spiritual awareness through the soul into the flowering of the intellect.

Paul had a subtle mind, a massive intellect and a developed soul. The following passage shows that he was familiar with the Greek philosophers as well as the Hebraic: "For the Jews require a sign and the Greeks seek after wisdom." The Jewish people were emotional, the Greeks intellectual. The Jews reacted through feeling, the Greeks by reason and logic. The Jews sought a sign, something that their emotion could feed on, while the Greeks sought a wisdom that would satisfy their intellects.

Paul condemned neither but by-passed both by saying, "We preach Christ crucified, unto the Jews a stumblingblock, and unto the Greeks foolishness; But unto them which are called, both Jews and Greeks, Christ the power of God, and the wisdom of God." The Jews had thought of God as an over-dwelling presence, and they were right. The Greeks had thought of the divine patterns or prototypes at the center of everything, and they were right.

Jesus taught the union of both. He combined the idea of an overdwelling Spirit, which was held by the Jews, with the Logos, or the Word, which was held by the Greeks. It was the putting of these two ideas together that was a stumblingblock to the Jews and foolishness to the Greeks. It was to the genius of Jesus that this great truth came full-orbed. This was his gospel—the glad tidings that the Kingdom of Heaven is at hand; that God has never been separated from the son and the son has never been separated from the Father.

". . . your faith should not stand in the wisdom of men, but in the power of God." It is a wisdom which Paul said the princes of this world do not have. It is "the wisdom of God in a mystery, even the hidden wisdom." Speaking of the spiritual universe he said, "Eye hath not seen, nor ear heard, neither have entered into the heart of man, the things which God hath prepared for them that love him. But God hath revealed them unto us by his Spirit . . ."

There is a spiritual vision which is not of this world. Spiritual things must be spiritually perceived through that "which the Holy Ghost teacheth; comparing spiritual things with spiritual. But the natural man receiveth not the things of the Spirit of God: for they are foolishness unto him: neither can he know them, because they are spiritually discerned."

Paul tells us that we may discern these spiritual things because "we have the mind of Christ." The essence of his instruction is a discernment of the spiritual universe in which we live. Because it is spiritual it must be spiritually understood. We can understand it because the mind of Christ is in us.

What could seem more foolish to the average intellect than the belief that we are living in a spiritual universe here and now? What could seem a greater stumblingblock to our ordinary intelligence than the belief that we now have that mind which was also in Christ? What could be more contrary to facts than to judge independently of such facts?

To what other mind than that of Jesus had come

the courage, the conviction and insight to proclaim
the unity of God with man in the face of everything
that appears so disunited? It is no wonder Paul referred to it as a mystery hid from the foundations of
the world, fully revealed in the glorious life, the
marvelous words and works of Jesus.

Those who believe in the teaching of the Master
and seek to follow his example receive a comfort and
an assurance that has come to no others. To those
who earnestly strive to follow the teaching of him
who spake as no man ever spoke before, what great
revelation must lie in store. Would that the imagination might catch the fire of the feeling of his words,
the intellect grasp their meaning, while the heart
gives full consent to the union of the human with the
Divine, here and now.

The Apostle said that he could speak to his followers only "as unto babes in Christ," telling them
that he had fed them with milk and not with meat.
Was he withholding the real meaning of the teaching of Christ, or merely giving it to them in a way
they could understand? This must have been the
case. He must have understood the esoteric meaning
of the teaching of Jesus. For after saying, "I have
planted, Apollos watered; but God gave the increase," he adds, "Now he that planteth and he that
watereth are one: and every man shall receive his
own reward, according to his own labour. For . . . ye

are God's building . . . Know ye not that ye are the temple of God, and that the Spirit of God dwelleth in you?" There is one life, that life is God, that life is our life now. He that plants and he that waters is one, and the God who gives the increase, operating through what is planted and what is watered, is one.

Moses, the great lawgiver, said that in due time God would raise up another like unto him who would complete his teaching. When this other came, proclaiming love as well as law, he completed the greatest system of spiritual philosophy ever given to the world—a combination of love and law, a union of the personal with the impersonal, an impulsion of love and a propulsion of law.

"And they shall be all taught of God." The final guidance of the soul is to that gentle urging from within, that intuition which always is in touch with the Spirit. This is the meaning of coming unto the Father through the son, and explains why it is that there is no mediator between God and man except Christ—Christ in us, the hope of glory, Emmanuel or God-with-us.

It was this interior awareness to which Jesus listened, making God real to him, giving him a conscious partnership with the Infinite, and making him able to speak as no other human being ever spoke before or since.

CHAPTER XII

Life Everlasting

ONE day when Jesus was talking with his followers he received news that Lazarus, one of his close friends, was very ill. According to the narrative, he deliberately waited until Lazarus died before he said, "Let us go unto him."

Arriving at the tomb of his friend, Jesus was confronted by Martha, a sister of Lazarus, who said, "Lord, if thou hadst been here my brother had not died." He replied, "Thy brother shall rise again." Martha answered that Lazarus would rise at the resurrection, but Jesus told her, "I am the resurrection and the life, and though a man be dead, yet shall he live." He was preparing his followers for the event that was to follow. He was going to prove that the Spirit cannot die, that man is an eternal being.

At this supreme moment he turned from all outward appearances, and commanding them to take away the stone, lifted up his soul and said, "Father,

I thank thee that thou hast heard me, and I know that thou hearest me always." Perhaps this is a perfect formula for us to use in resurrecting ourselves from past experiences, to roll away the stone, the block, the barrier, the so-hard and real facts which have entombed us.

The Enlightened One did not ask God to roll away the stone. This is an act that even God cannot do for us. It is left for us to roll away the stone of unbelief, and give thanks for the miracle which is about to happen. We must remove the barriers that keep life from flowing through us. We cannot put the life there, for while we are co-partners with it we are not creators of it. We are the beneficiaries of life, not its cause. We live because life is. We take life out, we do not put it in.

Lifting up his eyes Jesus said, "Father, I thank thee that thou hast heard me." This was a recognition of the universal Source of being. It was an acknowledgment of its reality and its presence. It was a complete acceptance. "I thank thee that thou hast heard me, and I know that thou hearest me always." Doubt and uncertainty are cast aside. There is a complete abandonment of the human to the Divine, a willingness to look into the tomb of the past without fear. There is an exaltation of spirit through the realization of the Divine Presence, not outside, but in, the tomb.

At the center of confusion there is peace. At the center of doubt there is certainty. At the center of death there is life. It was life and not death that Jesus recognized. And he recognized it where death appeared to be. Having lifted up his soul unto life he turned and commanded Lazarus to come forth.

We all have made tombs for ourselves. We have bound ourselves by fear, superstition and unbelief, and lain down in our self-created graves in a state of stupor, in a state of death. And yet, outside our tombs of self-imprisonment there is always a voice saying, "Arise and come forth!"

We must pass from death into life. Paul tells us that those who are resurrected from sin into salvation through Christ die no more. He implies that something about us dies daily, but yet, that which dies is not the spirit but the sin which is of the flesh. There can be but one real death and that is the dying of unreality to reality.

Because there is always an echo of the Spirit in our intellect, something within us is ever struggling toward the light. This conflict goes on in every man's mind. "For the good that I would I do not: but the evil which I would not, that I do." And again he says, "Now if I do that I would not, it is no more I that do it, but sin that dwelleth in me."

It was this fine differentiation between the eternal

Reality within and our mistakes that marks Paul as one who had spiritual insight. He could not have understood the message of Jesus unless he had been able to see that the human is struggling toward the Divine while the Divine is lifting the human up into its own awareness. "For I delight in the law of God after the inward man: But I see another law in my members, warring against the law of my mind, and bringing me into captivity . . . O wretched man that I am! who shall deliver me from the body of this death?"

It was Paul's belief that the hope of deliverance from our mistakes comes through a conscious union with Christ in God. For he said, "There is therefore now no condemnation to them which are in Christ Jesus . . . for the law of the Spirit . . . hath made me free from the law of sin and death." This is the triumph of the Spirit. It is the freedom which comes through conscious communion with Life. "For what the law could not do, in that it was weak through the flesh . . . the Spirit of him that raised up Jesus from the dead . . . shall also quicken your mortal bodies by his Spirit that dwelleth in you."

This calls for a complete turning of the mind to the Spirit of Christ within us. The Apostle tells us that "the Spirit itself beareth witness with our spirit, that we are the children of God." It is this inner witness of the Spirit that lifts us from the thralldom of flesh to Divine Sonship, which Paul likens unto "heirs of God and joint heirs with Christ."

He compares the sufferings through which we go in search after the Spirit as "not worthy to be compared with the glory which shall be revealed in us . . . Because the creature itself also shall be delivered from the bondage of corruption into the glorious liberty of the children of God . . . For whom he did foreknow, he also did predestinate to be conformed to the image of his Son . . . If God be for us who can be against us?" The Spirit is always triumphant, the Spirit foreknows and predestines complete salvation. Because the Spirit is for us, nothing can be against us.

Paul had received spiritual illumination. The light of heaven had fallen across his pathway. He had surrendered himself to this light and walked in it. He had found the relationship between Christ, the Universal Son, and each individual member of this Sonship. Through some divine inward awareness he had come to know that though we die daily because of our mistakes, we are daily resurrected by the indwelling Spirit, which is Christ.

"Who shall separate us from the love of Christ? shall tribulation, or distress, or persecution, or famine, or nakedness, or peril, or sword?" "Nay," says Paul, "in all these things we are more than con-

querors through him that loved us. For I am persuaded, that neither death, nor life, nor angels, nor
principalities, nor powers, nor things present, nor
things to come, nor height, nor depth, nor any other
creature, shall be able to separate us from the love of
God."

". . . now it is high time to awake out of sleep:
for now is our salvation nearer than we believed."
In this passage he implies that we are in a deep sleep
from which we must awake; we are in a hypnotic
state from which we must become aroused. We find
the same thought in one of the older prophets of
Israel: "Awake, thou that sleepest, and arise from
among the dead, and Christ shall give thee light."
And Jesus said, "Lazarus is asleep. I go to awaken
him." The material man is asleep and fails to recognize how close he is to the spiritual man. "For now
is our salvation nearer than we believed. The night
is far spent, the day is at hand."

Should we not arouse ourselves as from a long
night of sleep during which we have dreamed much
that is contrary to the nature of eternal truth? It is
certain that the natural man must awake to the spiritual. It is equally certain that the spiritual man is
right where we are. Our salvation is near at hand.

Spiritual powers are around and within us but we
are asleep to them. Now comes the touch of intuition
causing a restlessness, but mostly only a half-awaken-

ing, and we soon fall back into our stupor. We all have these moments. They come sometimes out of deep grief, sometimes in the midst of confusion, sometimes through meditation and prayer. There is no normal person living who has not at times half awakened from his stupor. Some, like Jesus, have completely wakened and never again fallen back into the stupor of separation from the center and source of their being.

Paul says that the night is far spent, the day is at hand; that we should "cast off the works of darkness and put on the armor of light." The armor of light suggests a radiance in which darkness cannot exist. This full armor of light with which we should surround ourselves is not something we assume or acquire. It is that which is. There is a light that lights every man's pathway. This light is not a personal accomplishment or a reward for endeavor. Like life itself, it is that which is. But it must be accepted.

Darkness is penetrated through love which leads to light. This love is more than a sentiment. It is that love arrived at through a deep realization of the unity of all things, the oneness of God with man and the oneness of man with man. "So we being many are one body in Christ, and every one members one of another."

The spiritual perception of unity is all-inclusive. Nothing that is real is separate from the Kingdom of Heaven. In such degree as our consciousness becomes actively unified with God it takes into itself, in some mystical manner which the intellect cannot explain, all that is. It is self-evident that Divinity must include humanity, even though humanity seeks to exclude Divinity. The larger circle will include the smaller and the two will become one—"that they might be one, even as we are one."

This is the meaning of being one with God in Christ and members of each other. The biggest life is the one that includes the most. The far horizon of the soul must not be obscured by barriers. There is no exclusion in the life that includes all. There is no such thing as a half unity.

Paul tells us that in seeking to realize this whole we should not be too concerned over non-essentials. "Let not him that eateth despise him that eateth not." He tells us that one man may esteem one day above another, while some esteem every day to be alike, but that each is "holden up for God is able to make him stand. Let every man be fully persuaded in his own mind . . . he that eateth, eateth to the Lord, for he giveth God thanks; and he that eateth not, to the Lord he eateth not, and giveth God thanks. For none of us liveth to himself, and no man dieth to himself."

He places the meaning of the act in its sincerity. Whether we fast or feast, if we do it unto God, in simplicity and faith, then God causes us to stand. It is the simplicity and the sincerity that count. We live by what is right and not because of the wrong that operates through us. No one can live to himself because he must live to the whole, to God. "For whether we live, we live unto the Lord; and whether we die, we die unto the Lord: whether we live therefore, or die, we are the Lord's."

This is a comprehensive statement of our relationship to life. It by-passes all barriers. It discovers God in the act which is to God. Whether we live or whether we die, we belong to life. Whether we go forth or return, we cannot stray from the unity of our soul with the source of its being. Whether we fast or feast, pray or remain silent, the dance of life goes on. And if everything we do is done unto God, through love, we are in the rhythm of life, one with the pulsation of the eternal heartbeat. "For it is written, As I live, saith the Lord, every knee shall bow to me, and every tongue shall confess to God."

We live unto life and we die unto life. This is what Jesus imparted to us: the certainty of immortality and the continuity of the individual life, forever expanding. When he said to the thief who was crucified with him, "To day shalt thou be with me in paradise," he was saying that the transition from this world to the next is immediate. We sleep from one life to awake to another.

Jesus deliberately spoke these words to the thief as one of the last and greatest of his lessons to humanity. The universe never holds anything against us and in any moment when we turn to it, it turns to us. The last moment is equal to the first because truth is a changeless and ever-present reality.

"Let not your heart be troubled. Ye believe in God; believe also in me." The Man of Compassion knew better than anyone else what the troubled heart means. He knew that self-preservation is a constant desire of the human mind. He had penetrated the veil between this world and the next and was able to function in either at will. The human Jesus loved his disciples. The Divine Christ knew that they would continue to live forever. Knowing that he was soon to leave them, and wishing to comfort them, he said, "In my Father's house are many mansions. If it were not so I would have told you. I go to prepare a place for you."

He was plainly telling his disciples that this world is but a temporary place; that we shall pass from this to another world. He was reiterating the ancient teaching of the eternal upward and spiralling evolution of the soul. He did not say, "This is one world and in the Kingdom of God there is another world. These two worlds constitute all there is to reality." He said exactly what we should have expected him to say, drawing from his well-spring of wisdom and inward experience: "In my Father's house are many mansions." Not one, not two, but many.

We cannot doubt that Jesus taught the eternal expansion of every soul. In the story of the prodigal, in the repeated gestures of forgiving people their sins and absolving them from their mistakes, and in his last act upon the cross, he was showing us that life is the gift of God; that somewhere, sometime, somehow, good will come alike to all. We may delay its advent. We may receive it only in part. But somewhere, through experience or by revelation, every soul will be compelled to accept the divine inheritance, to enter into the Father's house.

Jesus appeared after his physical death to show that the individual life goes on. It is not lost. It is not absorbed. It continues as it was. No sequence is broken. Therefore, he said that which is bound on earth is bound in heaven and that which is loosed on earth is loosed in heaven. We carry our consciousness with us across the borderline between this life and the next. After we die we are the same as we were before we passed from this world. The Wayshower said that state of existence is comparable to this: "I will drink no more of the fruit of the vine until I do it in my Father's house."

One plane reproduces another. "As above, so beneath; as below, so above." Things in the physical world are but copies of what is in heaven. Jesus was able to function on either plane at will. We shall miss the most significant part of his teaching unless we believe in his resurrection, and through this revelation, in the resurrection of all. Our world is but one of the "mansions" to which the Master referred. When we move from one mansion or experience into another we are not moving outside the Kingdom. We are progressively moving within it.

We should live as though we were in eternity now while at the same time realizing that the scenes of eternity are forever shifting. We shall never be caught in any one scene, for, if we were, our evolution would necessarily cease. But if we conceive of a body within a body, of the reproduction of this plane on the next, and at a higher level, there will be no confusion. There are bodies here and bodies there. As the Apostle said, "There are bodies celestial and bodies terrestrial. So also is the resurrection of the dead. The body is sown in weakness; it is raised in power. It is sown a natural body; it is raised a spiritual body, for there is both a natural body and a spiritual body."

The man who spoke these words was intimately acquainted with the teaching of Jesus and perhaps himself had penetrated the veil of the mystery of death. There is both a natural body and a spiritual body. When the natural body is laid down it is "sown in weakness" but the spiritual body is "raised in power." We do not carry this physical body into the next plane because Divine Wisdom has provided another body for that plane. The physical body is connected with the spiritual body which vitalizes it; the spiritual body never completely incarnates.

Nature has designed that when by any reason this physical instrument is no longer fit for the soul, then the spirit is severed from it. We should live as though we were immortal now. All fear of death should disappear and we should look forward to this final event with no sense of dread. It is just as natural to die to this life as it was to be born into it.

To those with faith such as Jesus had, death is of no consequence whatsoever. Often it comes as a release when the accumulated cares, burdens and fears of this life are laid down and a fresh beginning is made. We should not think of death as something to be longed for, neither should we think of it as something to be avoided.

Divine Wisdom has provided that when we enter this life we are met by loving friends who care for us. Speaking of the next life Jesus said, "I go to prepare a place for you." Divine Wisdom did not provide that transition from this world to the next be something we cannot comprehend, else it would have provided for our personal extinction. This concept the Great Teacher completely repudiated. If there is a continuity of the soul it must be one in which no threads are broken. Just as memory links yesterday with today, while anticipation extends to-day into tomorrow, so immortality is an unbroken continuity, a continual on-goingness in which the past is remembered, the present realized, and the future anticipated.

In the famous Fifteenth Chapter of I Corinthians, Paul tells of the resurrection of Jesus after which he "was seen of above five hundred brethren at once; of whom the greater part remain unto this present . . . After that, he was seen of James; then of all the apostles. And last of all he was seen of me also."

It was Paul, more than any other follower of Jesus, who put the philosophy of Christianity together. Following in the footsteps of the Master, Paul believed in the inner perfection of all creation, the unity of all life, and the immortality of the individual soul. He begins the greatest discourse on immortality ever written by saying that all the apostles had seen Jesus after his resurrection as well as hundreds of others. He himself had seen him at a later date. He was referring to his experience on the road to Damascus. All of this was in preparation for the message that was to follow.

"If in this life only we have hope in Christ, we are of all men most miserable. But now is Christ risen from the dead, and become the firstfruits of them that slept." To Paul, as to most of us, life would have no meaning if it ended with the grave. Even the glorious message of Jesus would be in vain and faith itself would be a mockery. But Paul assures us that Christ did rise from the dead and become the first fruits of them that slept.

The fruit of the sowing of this body in death is the resurrection of another body in eternal life. The Apostle makes so bold as to say that "by man came death, by man came also the resurrection of the dead. For as in Adam all die, even so in Christ shall all be made alive." This remarkable passage states that death is an invention of the human mind and that while all may go through the experience of dying, because of our ignorance of the true meaning of life, we shall all experience a resurrection from among the dead.

In saying that we die in Adam and are resurrected in Christ, Paul is speaking about the physical and the spiritual. It is the Adam in us that dies, not Christ. He says that the last enemy to be destroyed is death; that when all things shall become subject to the Spirit, death itself will cease even to be an experience. ". . . that God may be all in all."

"But some man will say, How are the dead raised up? and with what body do they come?" For thousands of years before Paul asked this question the spiritually illumined had taught that everything in this world is but a copy of what is in heaven, that there is an interior to things which is spiritual. Therefore, Paul, who was well versed in these teachings, said there are "celestial bodies and bodies terrestrial." He did not say there *shall be* a celestial body, but that one already exists. This is the inner, invisible body of pure Spirit, the body that is "over yonder" or in the Kingdom of Heaven within.

"So also is the resurrection of the dead . . . It (the body) is sown in weakness; it is raised in power: it is sown a natural body; it is raised a spiritual body. There is a natural body, and there is a spiritual body." The resurrection from among the dead is not changing from something which we are not into something which we are to become. It is a laying down of the physical body and an on-going with a spiritual body we already have.

"The first man is of the earth, earthy: the second man is the Lord from heaven." The first Adam is a living soul, the last Adam is a quickening spirit. The first Adam is of this earth, the second Adam is the Lord from heaven. This is the human and the Divine, the flesh and the Spirit.

But it might be asked, who is immortal? This question Jesus answered when he said that "he is not a God of the dead, but of the living, for in His sight all are alive." God is life and cannot will death. There is no death to the soul. It is only the unwise who believe that immortality belongs to one individual or group of individuals and not to others. There is nothing in this short life that anyone could do to earn immortality, as though it were a reward of merit. There is nothing anyone could do to destroy it if it already exists. Immortality is either a principle in nature or it has no existence. Everyone is immortal or no one is immortal. It does not necessarily follow that everyone is awake to his immortality.

Jesus said to the thief, "To day shalt thou be with me in paradise," and Paul said, "We shall not all sleep, but we shall all be changed. In a moment, in the twinkling of an eye . . ." It does not follow that this change need wait the advent of our physical death. Many live in such close communion with life that they are aware of immortality now and look forward to the laying down of this body as one looks forward to a journey.

When we enter this world we are welcomed with love and cared for with tender solicitation. If it is true that one plane reproduces another, and that heaven is but a continuation of earth, then we should expect to be met likewise by love and tender solicitation in the new life. Divine Wisdom has given us a memory which links one event with another, thus making possible a continuity of consciousness. This memory is non-physical. It is not stored up in the brain but in the mind itself. It is the mind, the consciousness, the spirit, the soul that is immortal, not the physical form.

The warmth and color of human personality, what we really love in people and that which responds to us, is non-physical and is in no way subject to this mortal body. This has now been thoroughly demonstrated and we need not even resort to faith for assurance because the facts have been proved. It is now known that the mind alone can reproduce the activities of the senses without using the sense organs. It can do this while retaining its memory of the past, being conscious of the present moment, and anticipating the future.

This is all immortality could mean: to know and to be known, to think, to be persons, independent of the physical body. It is written that no man has seen God, only the Son has revealed the Father. We do not see the Spirit, yet we live in It. An artist does not see beauty; he feels it. From what he feels he creates an object of his feeling which we call art. Beauty itself is subjective, the beautiful is objective. One is seen, the other felt. Thus the Bible says that the things which are seen are not made of the things which do appear.

Just as no one has seen God, the living Spirit, so no one has seen man, the spirit which lives in God. No one has seen truth or integrity, yet no one doubts their existence. The art, wit and science of man combined cannot see the mind of man. Yet we do not doubt that this mind exists. It is the Real Self, conscious of its own being and its environment, knowing and being known, remembering, experiencing and anticipating.

The warmth and color of physical personality is the essence of an invisible presence which dominates our days on earth and withdraws when the silver chord is broken and the spiritual body is severed from the physical. The physical returns to the dust whence it came and the spirit to the God who gave it. Our return to the Spirit is not a long journey but a quick awakening—" in a moment, in the twinkling of an eye," as Paul said. It is no wonder he exclaimed, "O death, where is thy sting? O grave, where is thy victory?"

As recorded in Acts, on the day of Pentecost, Peter ". . . standing up with the eleven, lifted up his voice," saying that Jesus had "loosed the pains of death: because it was not possible that he should be holden of it." Death has no power over life. Peter spoke of keeping the Lord always before his face, seeing the Spirit in everything, feeling Its presence in people and Its power in passing events. "Therefore did my heart rejoice, and my tongue was glad; moreover, also my flesh shall rest in hope." When good is continually held before our mental outlook the heart will rejoice, the tongue be made glad, and the flesh "rest in hope."

". . . thou wilt not leave my soul in hell, neither wilt thou suffer thine Holy One to see corruption." The statement: "Thou wilt not leave my soul in hell," is quite different from the idea that God might cast our souls into hell. Peter implies that the soul already is in purgatory until the day of its redemption, which is an awakening to the Spirit, that part of us which he said cannot see corruption. We are not cast into purgatory, but lifted out of it. There is nothing morbid in this. It is a joyful recognition of the emancipation that must come when we turn from evil to good.

We are to "count all things but loss" that we may "be found in him . . . Christ the righteousness which is of God by faith." It is through this being found in him that Paul said we "attain unto the resurrection of the dead." He was speaking of a resurrection which takes place here and now, and not later. He said that he had not fully attained this, but he added, "I follow after that I may apprehend that for which also I am apprehended." This is a repetition of his thought that we shall know even as we already are known.

According to Paul, none of us has completely done this but we should all strive toward it, and if we will follow those things "whereto we have already attained," we shall attain unto greater things. In order to do this we must think, act and live as though we were in the Kingdom of God. Pressing forward to this "high mark," keeping before us the glorious ideal of Jesus, we too shall enter into union with Christ.

Like the Christed One, Paul realized that this great attainment is through love and we see the tenderness of his heart where he says, "Therefore, my brethren dearly beloved and longed for, my joy and crown, so stand fast in the Lord, my dearly beloved . . . Rejoice in the Lord alway: and again I say, Rejoice," for "the Lord is at hand."

And through the whole process this great teacher tells us that "the peace of God, which passeth all understanding, shall keep your hearts and minds through Christ Jesus . . . Finally, brethren, whatsoever things are true, whatsoever things are honest, whatsoever things are just, whatsoever things are pure, whatsoever things are lovely, whatsoever things are of good report . . . think on these things."

Paul, like Jesus, tells us that out of the surrender of not-being to the All-Being, of the apparent having to the All-Giver, we shall not lose, but find, the Real Self. How can we be less if we think of more? How can we hate if we entertain love? How can we fear if we are filled with faith? How can we die if we know that life is eternal? Therefore, Paul says, ". . . God shall supply all your need according to his riches and glory in Christ Jesus." Shall not the greater contain the lesser while heaven holds earth in its soft embrace?

We should confidently look forward to those "many mansions" which Jesus spoke of, not as an idle dream or a beautiful word picture, but as an actual reality. We should have an enthusiastic anticipation of the more and the more and the more, not merely as an eternal hope but as an eternal recognition. Each new day may be looked forward to as a fresh adventure, a new beginning, another starting point in that endless progression of the soul which Jesus believed in, and which, by some divine intuition, we all sense. "World without end. Amen."